# MONET IN GIVERNY

## LANDSCAPES OF REFLECTION

*Edited by Benedict Leca*

cincinnati art museum

g

This catalog accompanies the exhibition *Monet in Giverny: Landscapes of Reflection* on display at the Cincinnati Art Museum from February 4, 2012 –May 13, 2012.



First published jointly in 2012 by GILES
An imprint of D Giles Limited
4 Crescent Stables,
139 Upper Richmond Road,
London SW15 2TN, UK
www.gilesltd.com

Library of Congress
Cataloging-in-Publication Data

Monet, Claude, 1840-1926.
Monet in Giverny : landscapes of reflection / organized and edited by
Benedict Leca ; essays by Lynne Ambrosini ... [et al.].
p. cm.
"This catalog accompanies the exhibition Monet in Giverny: Landscapes of Reflection on display at Cincinnati Art Museum from February 4, 2012-May 13, 2012."
Includes bibliographical references and index.
ISBN 978-1-907804-03-8 (pbk.)
1. Monet, Claude, 1840-1926--Exhibitions. 2. Landscapes in
art--Exhibitions. 3. Giverny (France)--In art--Exhibitions. I. Leca,
Benedict. II. Ambrosini, Lynne. III. Cincinnati Art Museum. IV. Title.

ND553.M7A4 2012
759.4--dc23

2011029094

ISBN: 978-1-907804-03-8



The exhibition was curated by Benedict Leca, Curator of European Painting, Sculpture, and Drawings, Cincinnati Art Museum

For the Cincinnati Art Museum:
Scott Hisey, Director of Design and Dissemination
Benedict Leca, Curator of European Painting, Sculpture, and Drawings
Anne Buening, Production Editor
Connie Newman, Retail Coordinator
Robert Deslongchamps, Head of Photo Services

For D Giles Limited:
Copy-edited and proof-read by Sarah Kane
Designed by Alfonso Iacurci
Produced by GILES, an imprint of D Giles Limited, London
Printed in Hong Kong

All titles are as specified by lender institutions.

All measurements are in inches and centimeters; height precedes width precedes depth.

Front and back cover: Claude Monet, *Waterlilies* (detail), 1903, oil on canvas, 32 x 40 in. (81.3 x 101.6 cm), The Dayton Art Institute, Gift of Mr. Joseph Rubin (1953.11)

Front flap: Nickolas Muray, *Claude Monet*, 1926, gelatin silver print, 10 x 8 in. (25.4 x 20.3 cm), Courtesy of George Eastman House, International Museum of Photography and Film, Gift of Mrs. Nickolas Muray (77:0188:2038) ©Nickolas Muray Photo Archives

Frontispiece: Nickolas Muray, *Claude Monet*, 1926, gelatin silver print, 10 x 8 in. (25.4 x 20.3 cm), Courtesy of George Eastman House, International Museum of Photography and Film, Gift of Mrs. Nickolas Muray (77:0188:2032) ©Nickolas Muray Photo Archives

# CONTENTS

# DIRECTOR'S FOREWORD

*Aaron Betsky*

Exactly at the moment when science made it clear to us that the world as we understood it in our mind was not the same as the world we knew through our senses, Claude Monet was finding in Giverny a universe to call and make his own. Complex, concrete, and yet infinite in its refractions, Giverny was reality as Monet would arrange and live it. As curator Dr. Benedict Leca points out in the current volume and exhibition, this painter found reflected in the ponds and rivers of his rural retreat an affirmation of a knowable as well as evocative universe, which he reflected in the paintings we cherish today.

In this focused examination of one of Monet's most seductive bodies of work, Dr. Leca has found not a dissolution of reality or a loss of personality in an endless miasma of color. Instead, he sees a reflection of objects brought together in the medium of water; the hubbub of modern life contained in the mirrored surfaces of a pond; and a self-portrait of the artist through layers of paint.

This study affirms both Monet's modernism and his individuality, and helps us see work we almost take for granted in a new manner. It is part of the Cincinnati Art Museum's attempt to contribute to our knowledge and enjoyment of great art through focused studies of small groups of paintings and artifacts. Spearheaded by Dr. Leca, this program is, in turn, part of the Art Museum's efforts to use its resources to create nodes of intense art experience, both through its exhibitions and through its public programs and publications.

We are very grateful to Dr. Leca for his scholarship and organizational talents, which have brought this project to fruition. We would also like to thank all of the lenders for their generosity in loaning these exceptional paintings, and all of the supporters of this project and the Art Museum more broadly.

# ACKNOWLEDGMENTS

The Cincinnati Art Museum wishes to thank the following for making the exhibition *Monet in Giverny: Landscapes of Reflection* possible:

**SPONSORS**

The Selz Foundation
Oliver Family Foundation

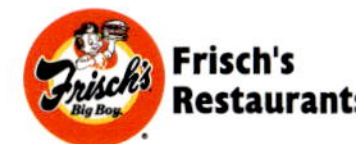


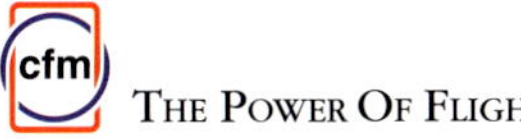


Bahl & Gaynor Investment Counsel
Fund Evaluation Group, LLC
In memory of Virginia Kreimer Faught
Mr. and Mrs. H.C. Buck Niehoff

In partnership with the European-American Chamber of Commerce, Cincinnati

**LENDING INSTITUTIONS**

Allen Memorial Art Museum, Oberlin College; Columbus Museum of Art; The Dayton Art Institute; Denver Art Museum; Museum of Fine Arts, Boston; Museum of Fine Arts, Houston; Philadelphia Museum of Art; Private Collection

Organizers wish to thank the following: Molly Ott Ambler, Edgar Peters Bowron, Anne Cappel, Marjorie B. Cohn, Lee Cowan, Leora Maltz-Leca, Emily Rauh Pulitzer, George T.M. Shackelford, Dr. Edward Silberstein, Will South, Timothy Standring, Dominique Vasseur, and the entire Cincinnati Art Museum staff, especially curatorial assistant Anne Buening.

The Cincinnati Art Museum gratefully acknowledges the generous operating support provided by ArtsWave, the Ohio Arts Council, and the City of Cincinnati, as well as our members.

This exhibition is supported by an indemnity from the Federal Council on the Arts and the Humanities.

# CATALOG



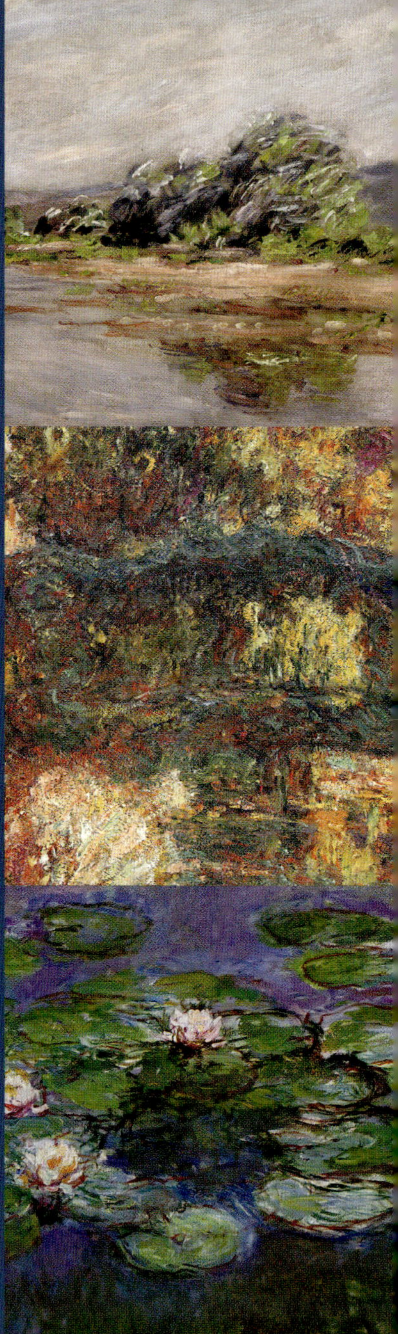

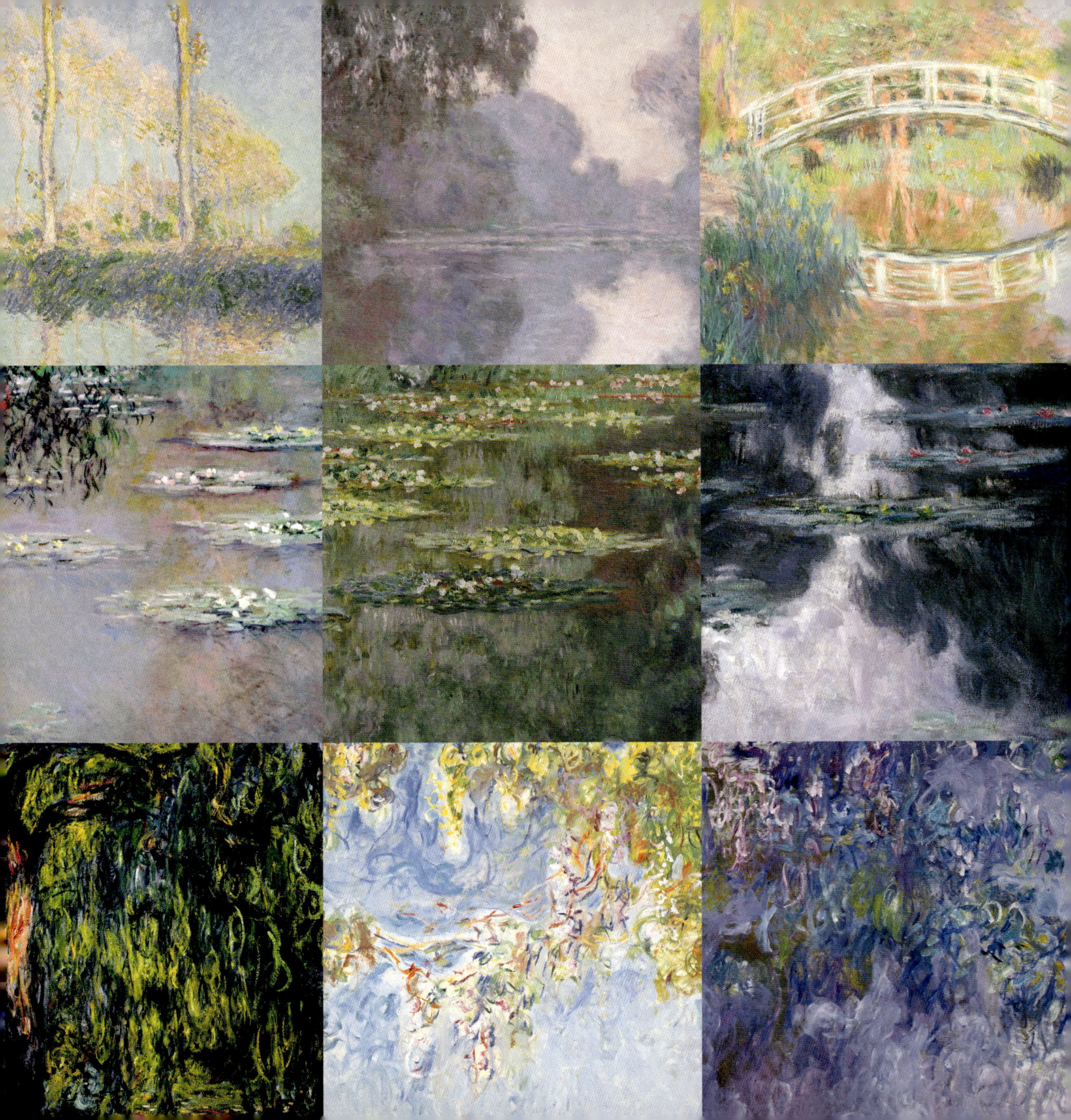

CAT 1

*The Seine at Port-Villez (A Gust of Wind) (La Seine à Port-Villez (Le Coup de vent))*
1883–90, oil on canvas,
23 ¾ × 39 ¼ in. (60.3 × 99.7 cm)

Columbus Museum of Art, Ohio: Gift of Howard D. and Babette L. Sirak, the Donors to the Campaign for Enduring Excellence, and the Derby Fund (1991.001.043)

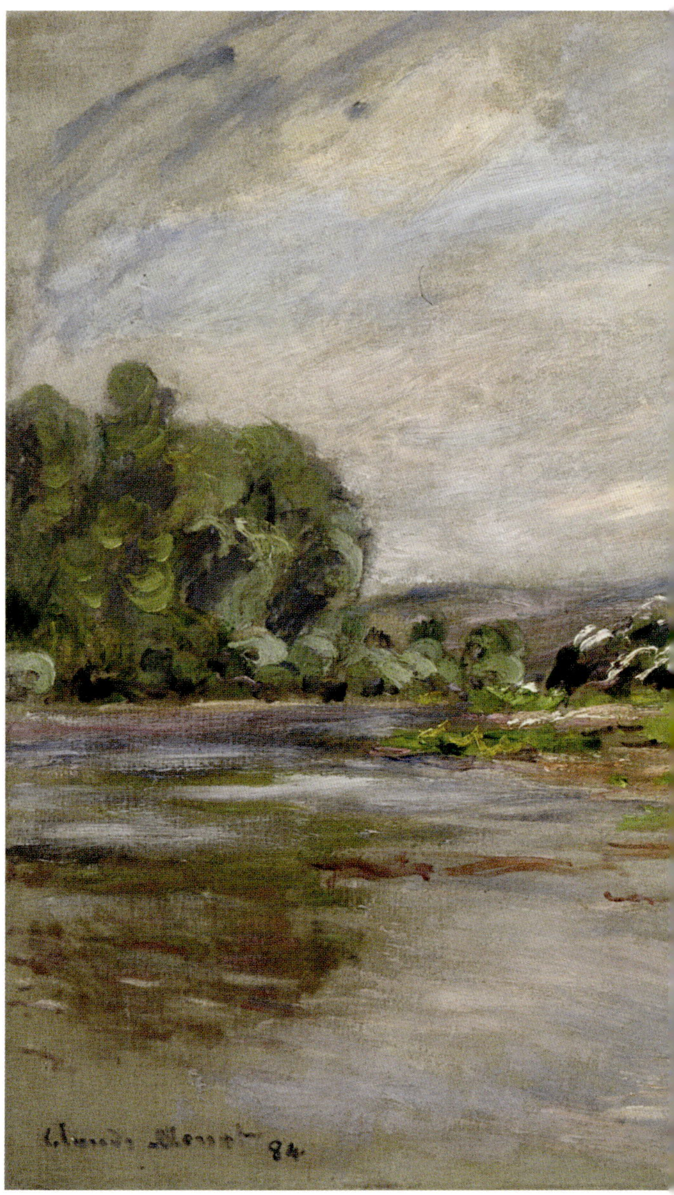

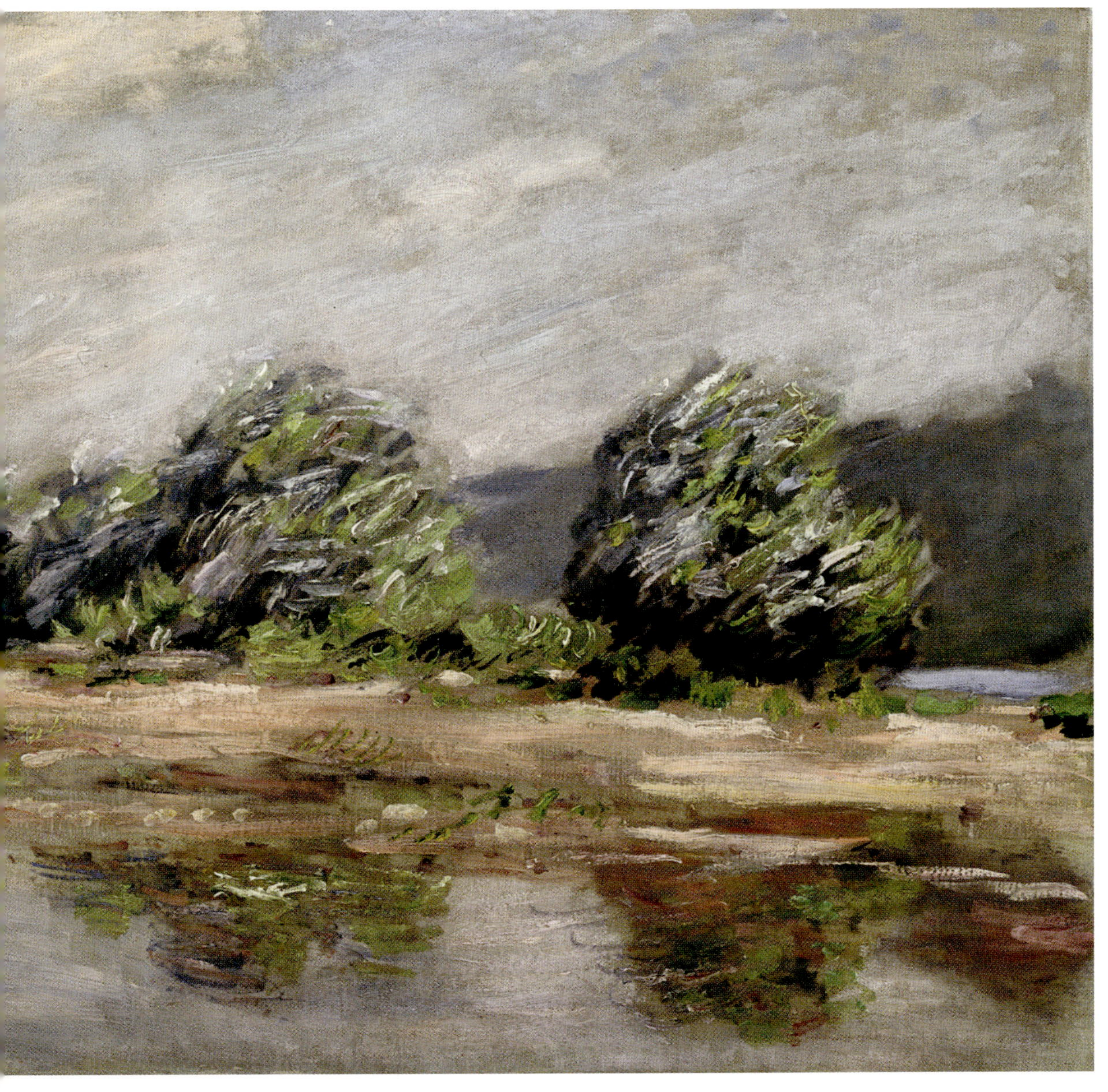

**CAT 2**

*Poplars*
1891, oil on canvas,
36 ⅝ × 29 $^{3}/_{16}$ in. (93 × 74.1 cm)

Philadelphia Museum of Art:
The Chester Dale Collection,
1951 (1951-109-1)

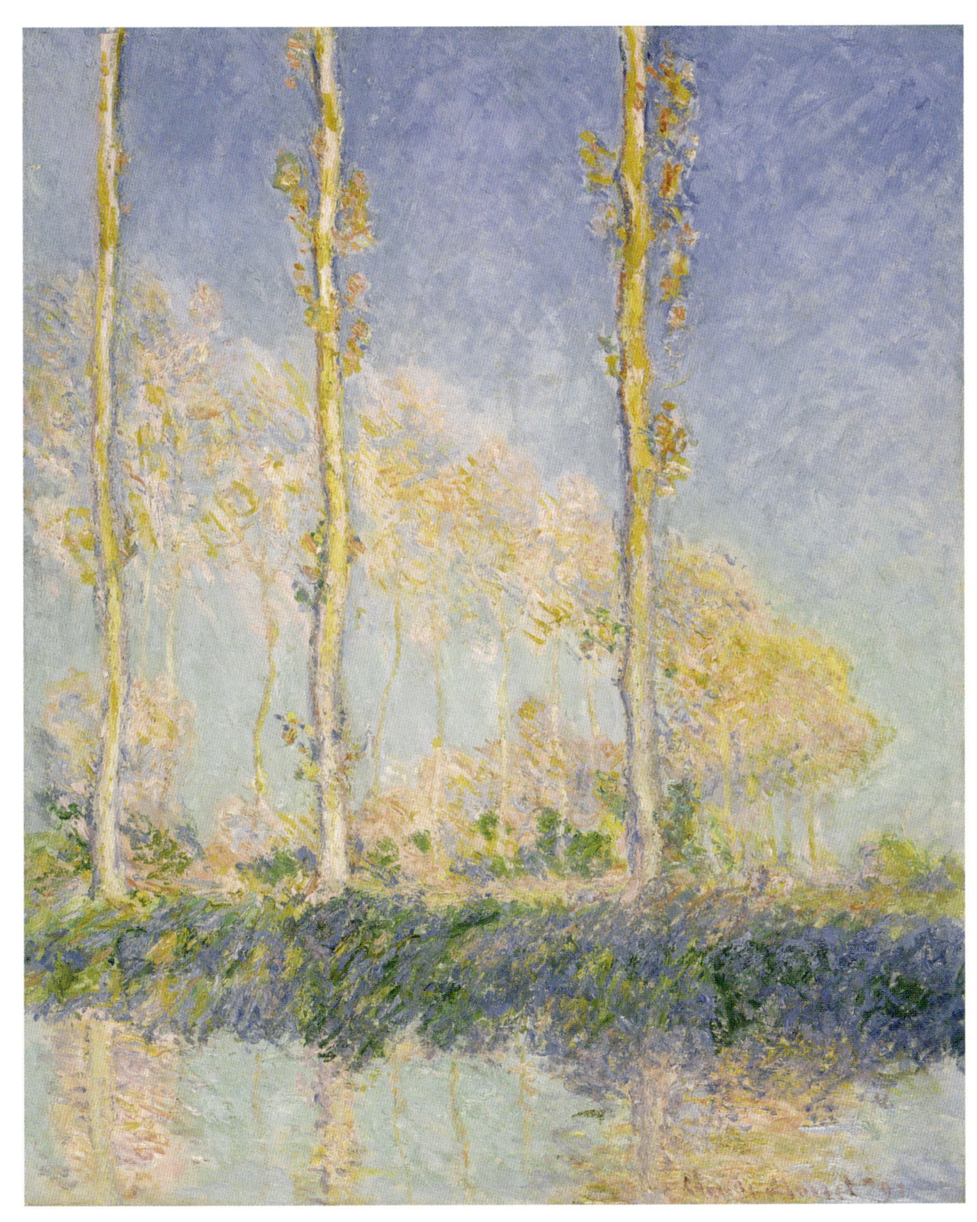

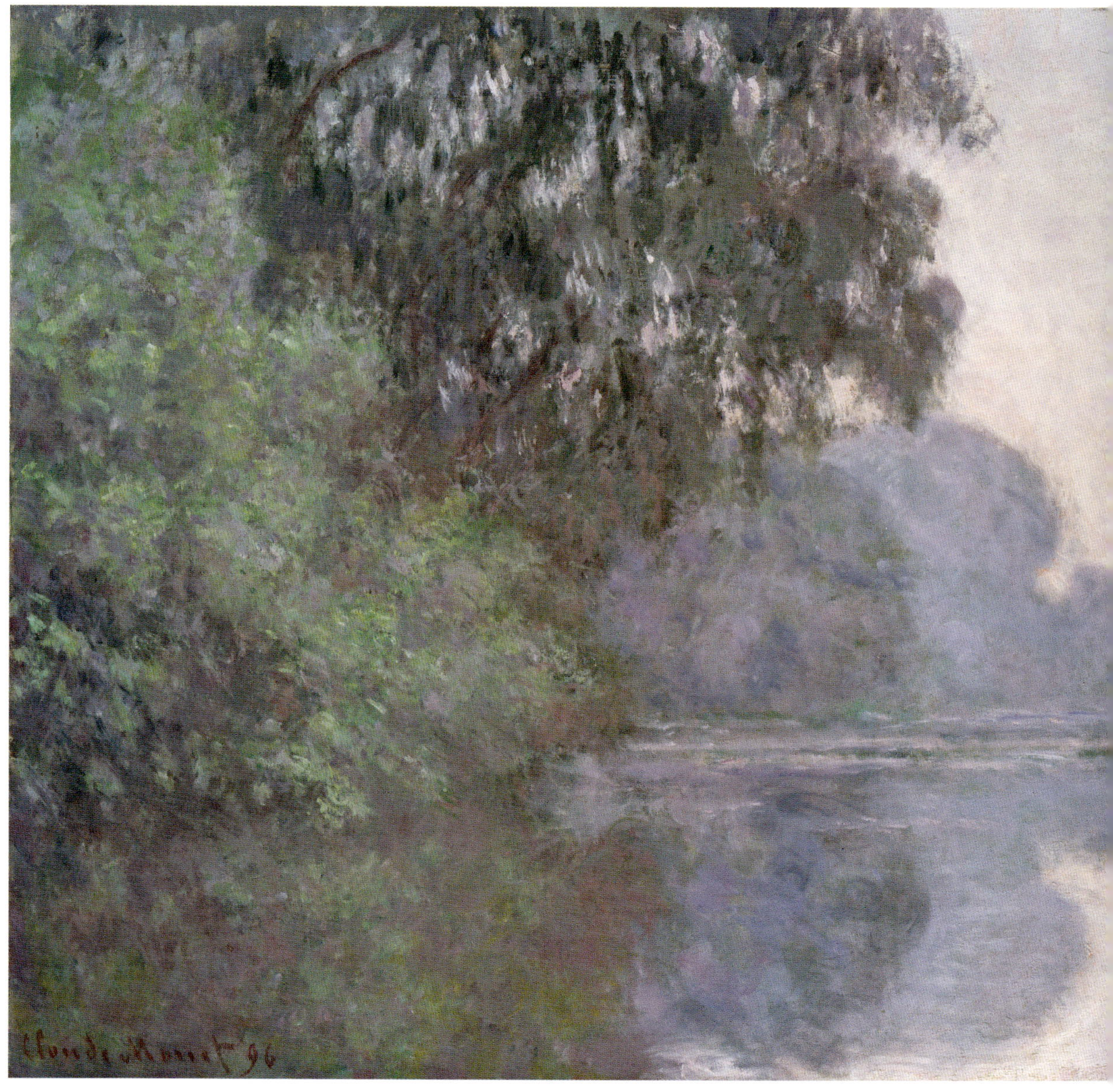

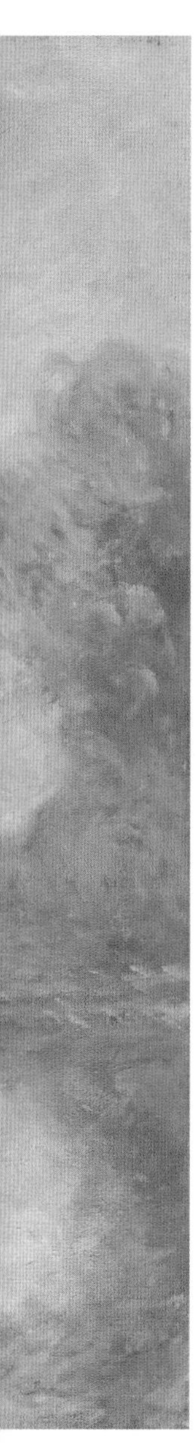

**CAT 3**

*Morning on the Seine,*
*near Giverny*
1896, oil on canvas,
29 × 36 ⅝ in. (73.7 × 93 cm)

Museum of Fine Arts, Boston:
Juliana Cheney Edwards
Collection (39.655)

**CAT 4**

*Japanese Footbridge, Giverny*
1895, oil on canvas,
31 × 38 ½ in. (78.7 × 97.8 cm)

Philadelphia Museum of Art: Gift of F. Otto Haas, and partial gift of the reserved life interest of Carole Haas Gravagno, 1993 (1993-151-2)

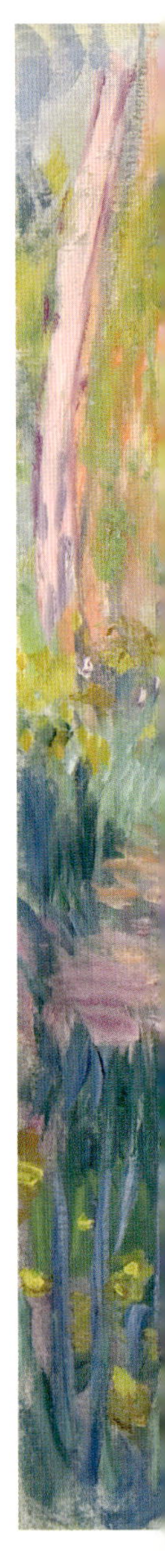

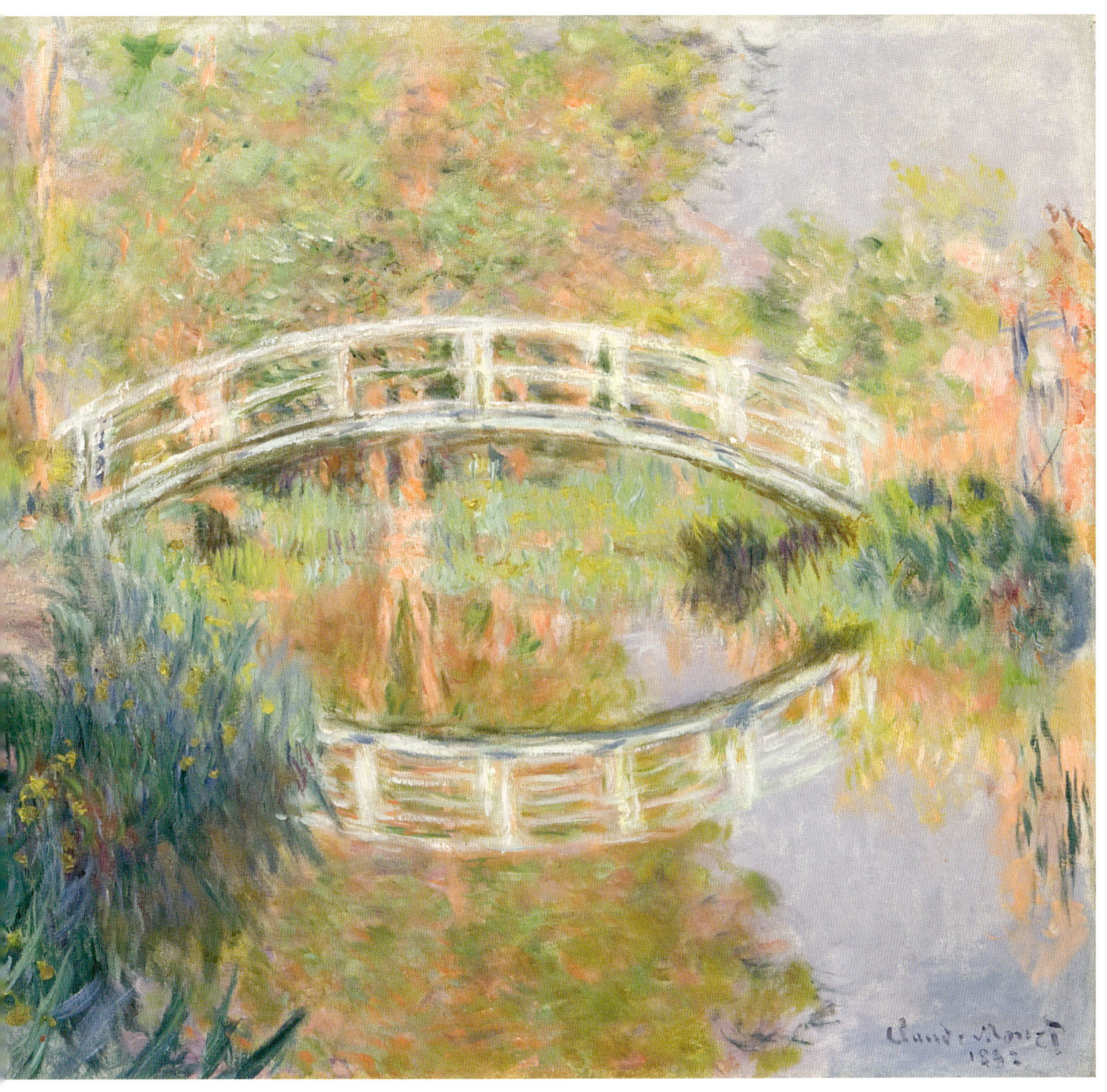

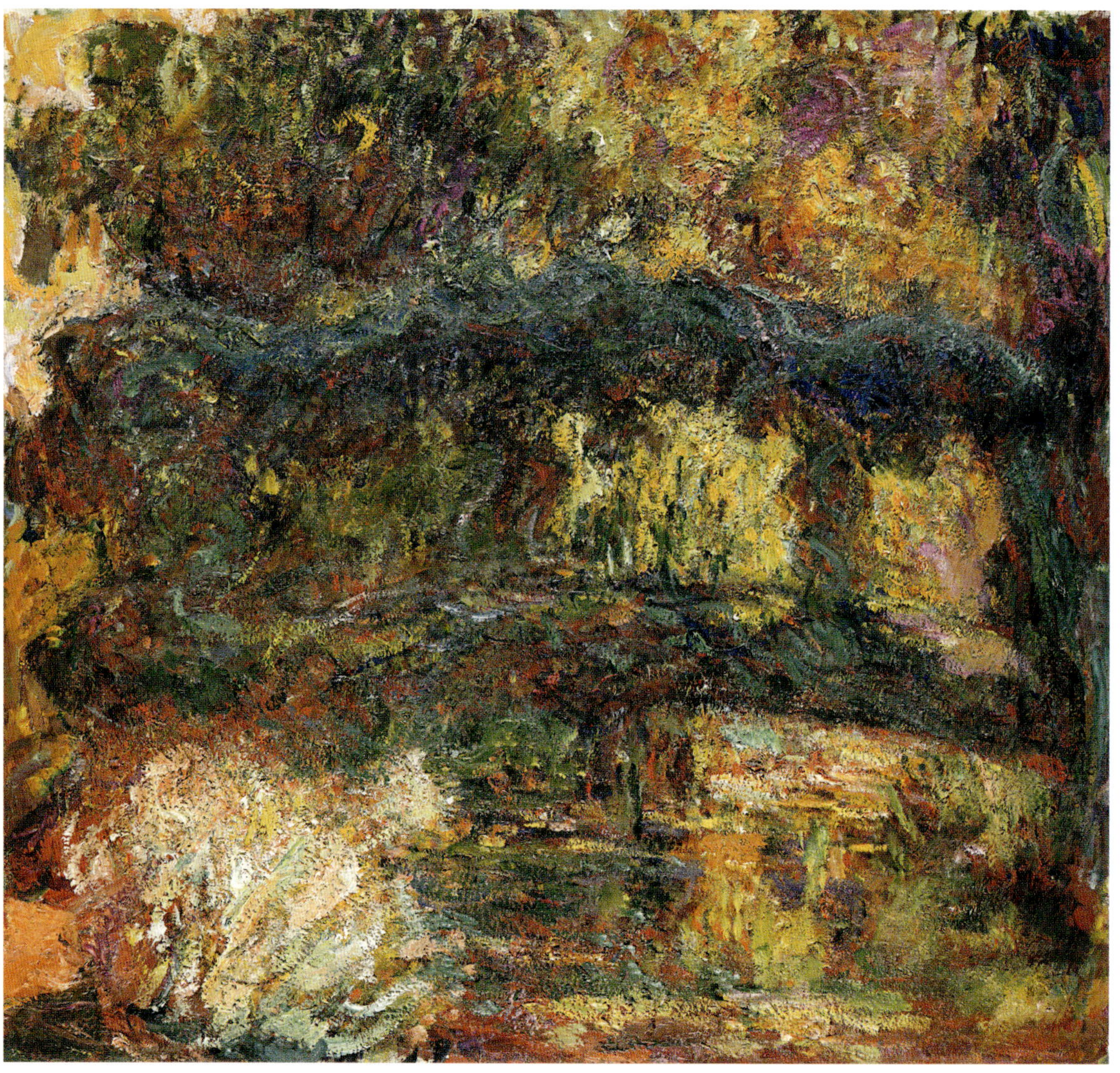

**CAT 5**

*Nympheas, Japanese Bridge*
1918–26, oil on canvas,
35 × 36 ½ in. (88.9 × 92.7 cm)

Philadelphia Museum of Art:
The Albert M. Greenfield
and Elizabeth M. Greenfield
Collection, 1974 (1974-178-38)

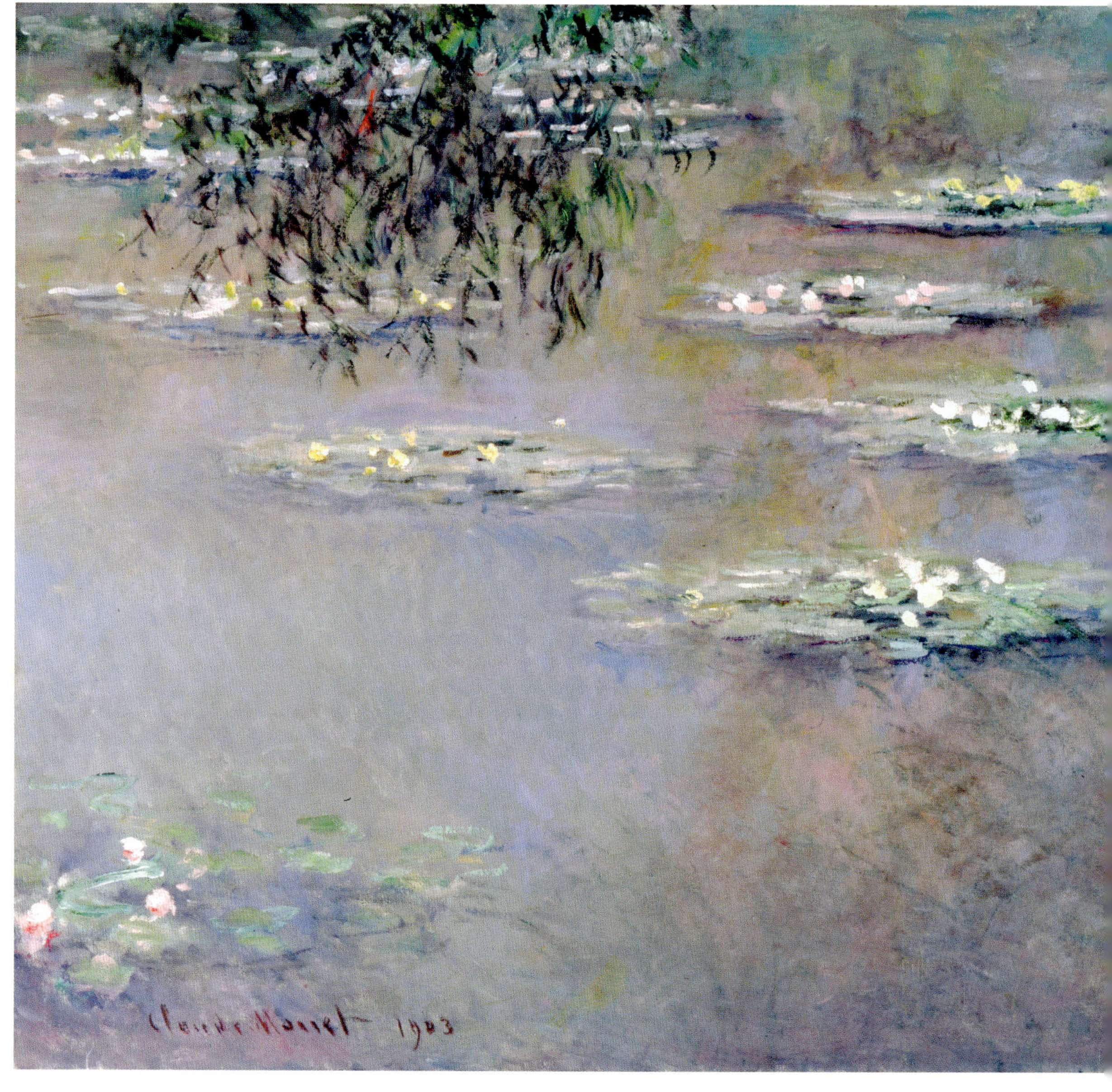
Claude Monet 1903

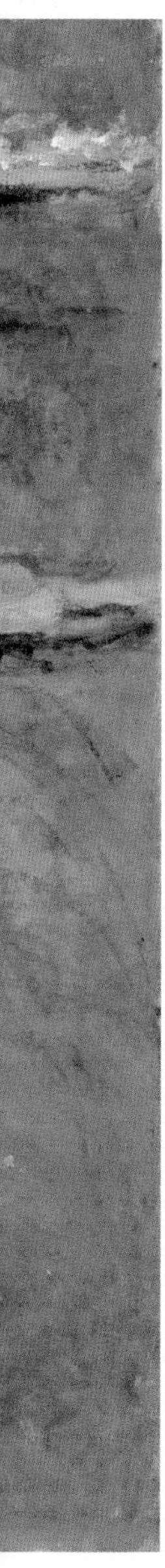

**CAT 6**

*Waterlilies*
1903, oil on canvas,
32 × 40 in. (81.3 × 101.6 cm)

The Dayton Art Institute:
Gift of Mr. Joseph Rubin
(1953.11)

**CAT 7**

*Le Bassin des Nymphéas*
1904, oil on canvas,
35 ⅛ × 36 5/16 in. (89.2 × 92.3 cm)

Denver Art Museum Collection:
Funds from Helen Dill Bequest
(1935.14)

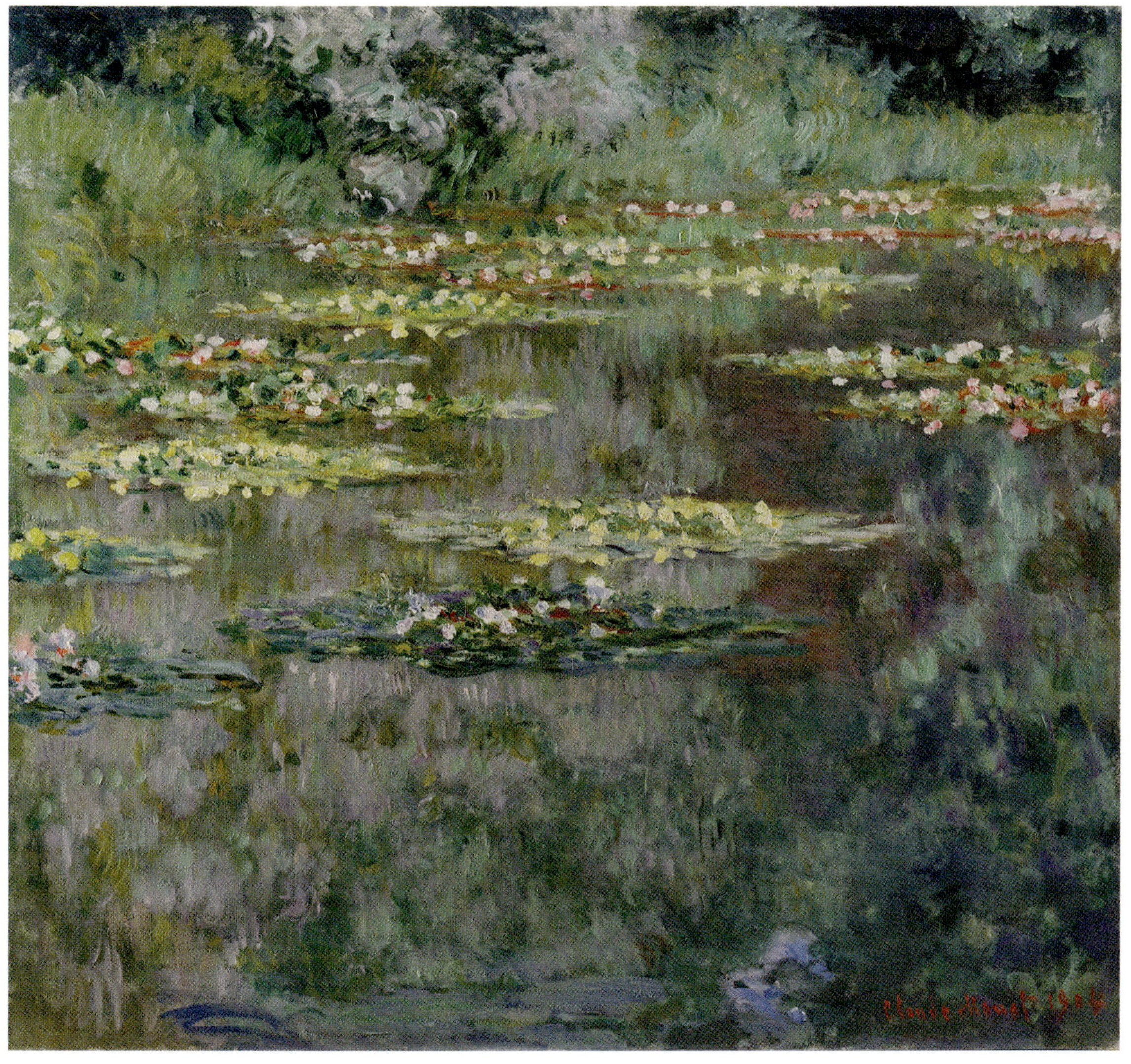

**CAT 8**

*Water Lilies (Nymphéas)*
1907, oil on canvas,
36 ¼ × 31 ¹⁵⁄₁₆ in. (92.1 × 81.2 cm)

The Museum of Fine Arts,
Houston: Gift of Mrs.
Harry C. Hanszen (68.31)

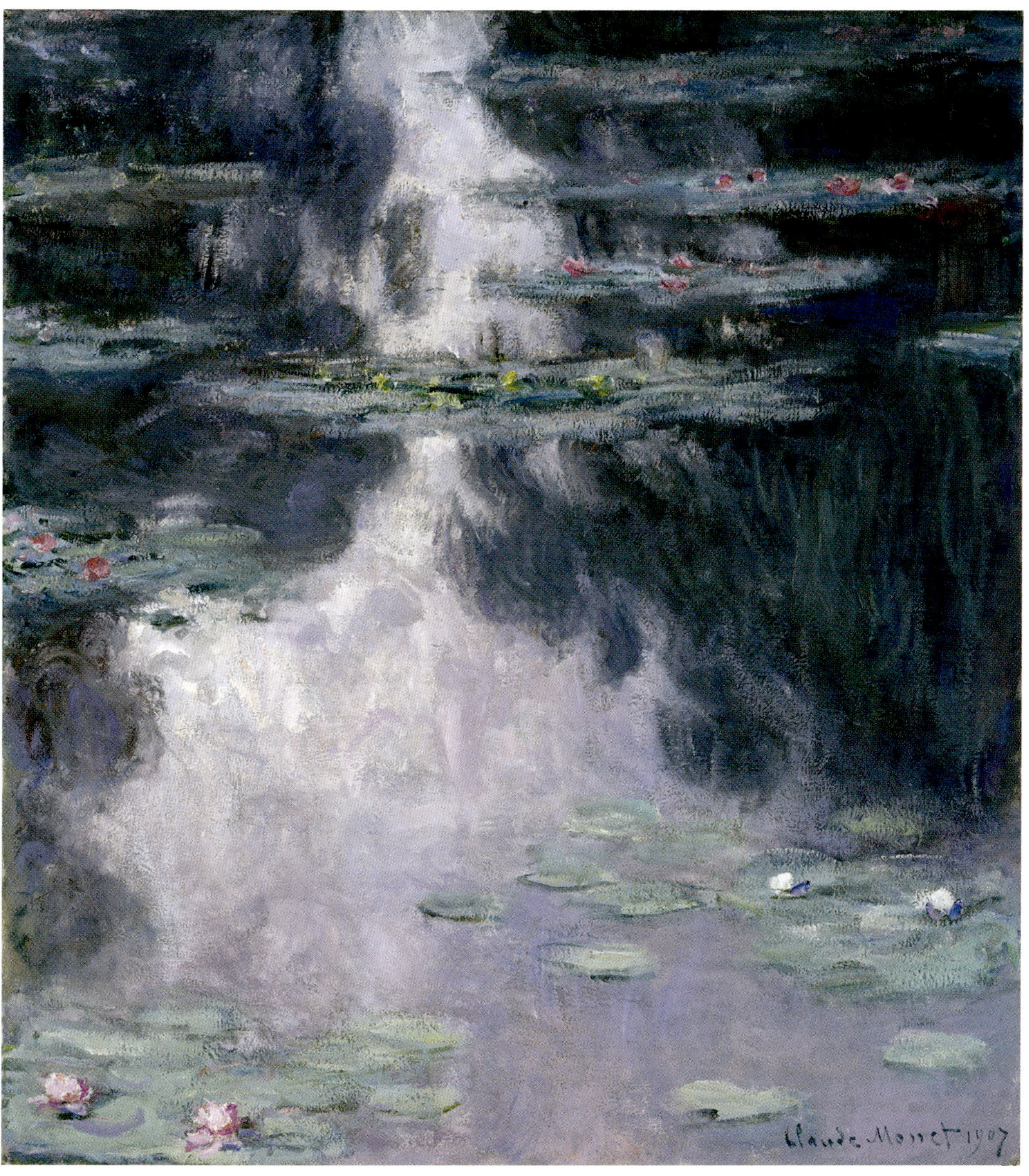
Claude Monet 1907

**CAT 9**

*Water Lilies*
ca. 1916–19, oil on canvas,
51 ⅛ × 78 ⅞ in. (129.9 × 200.3 cm)

Private Collection

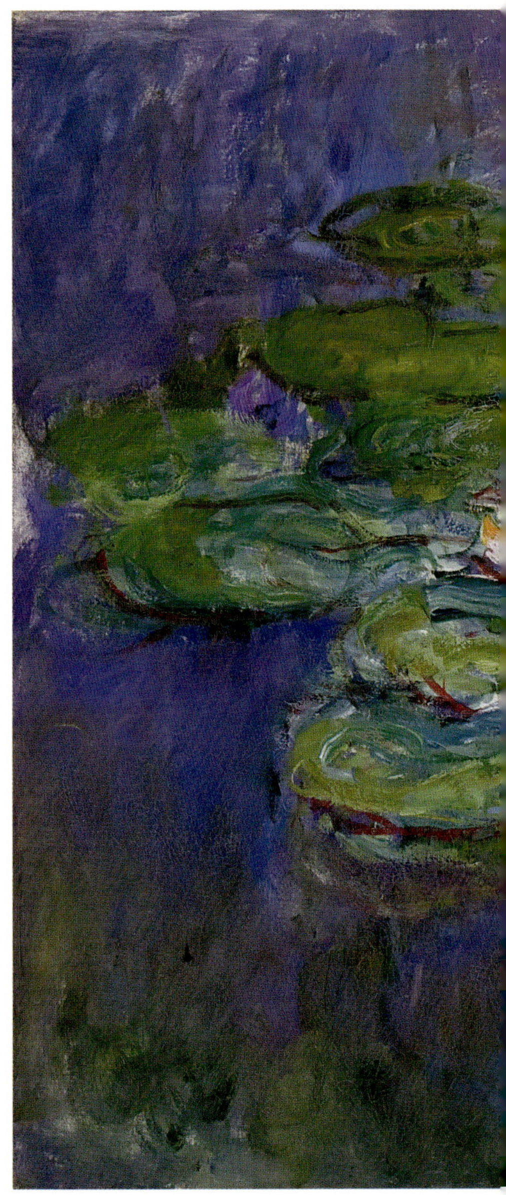

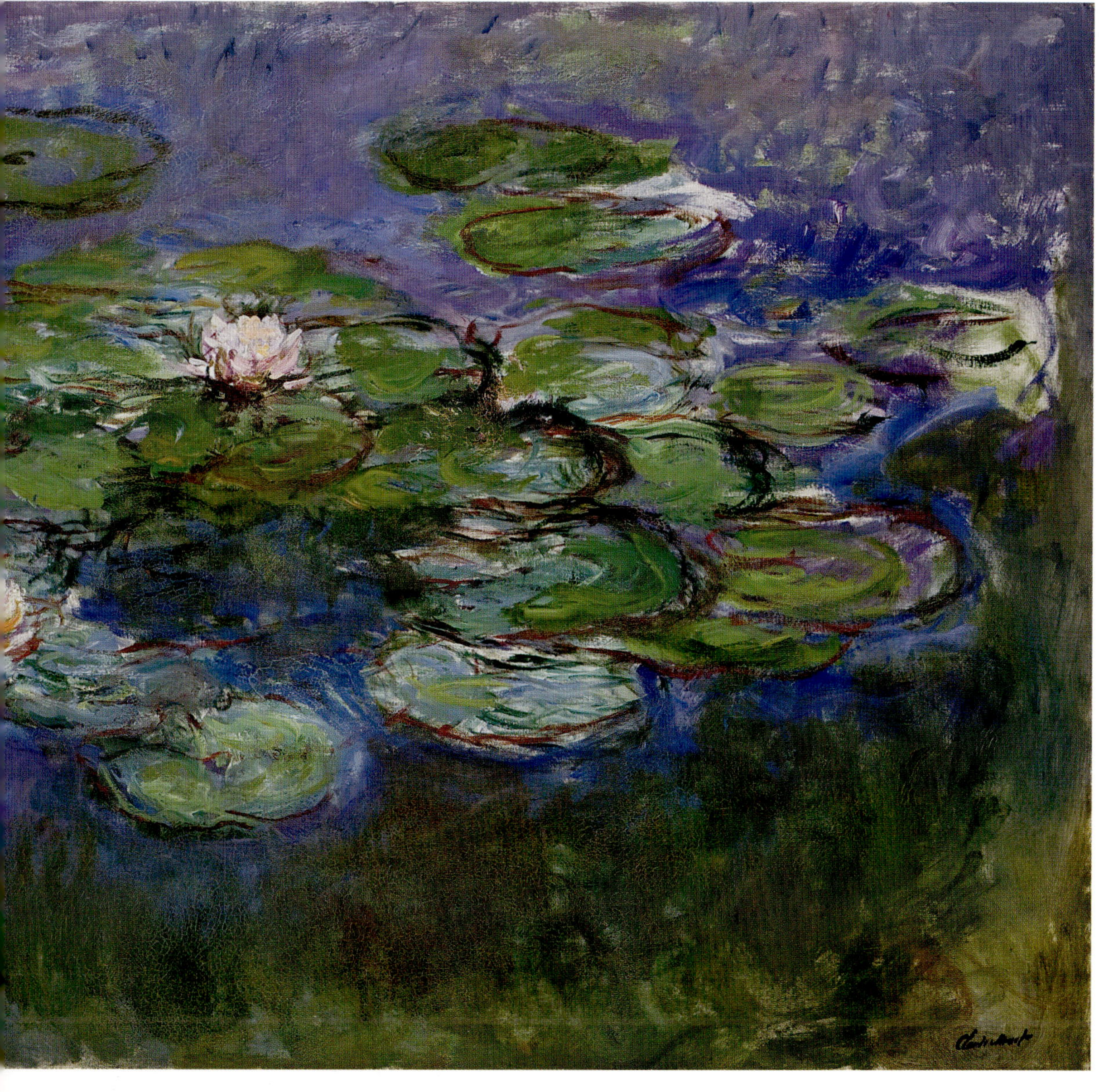

**CAT 10**

*Weeping Willow (Saule pleureur)*
1918, oil on canvas,
51 ⅝ × 43 7⁄16 in. (131 × 110.3 cm)

Columbus Museum of Art, Ohio: Gift of Howard D. and Babette L. Sirak, the Donors to the Campaign for Enduring Excellence, and the Derby Fund (1991.001.041)

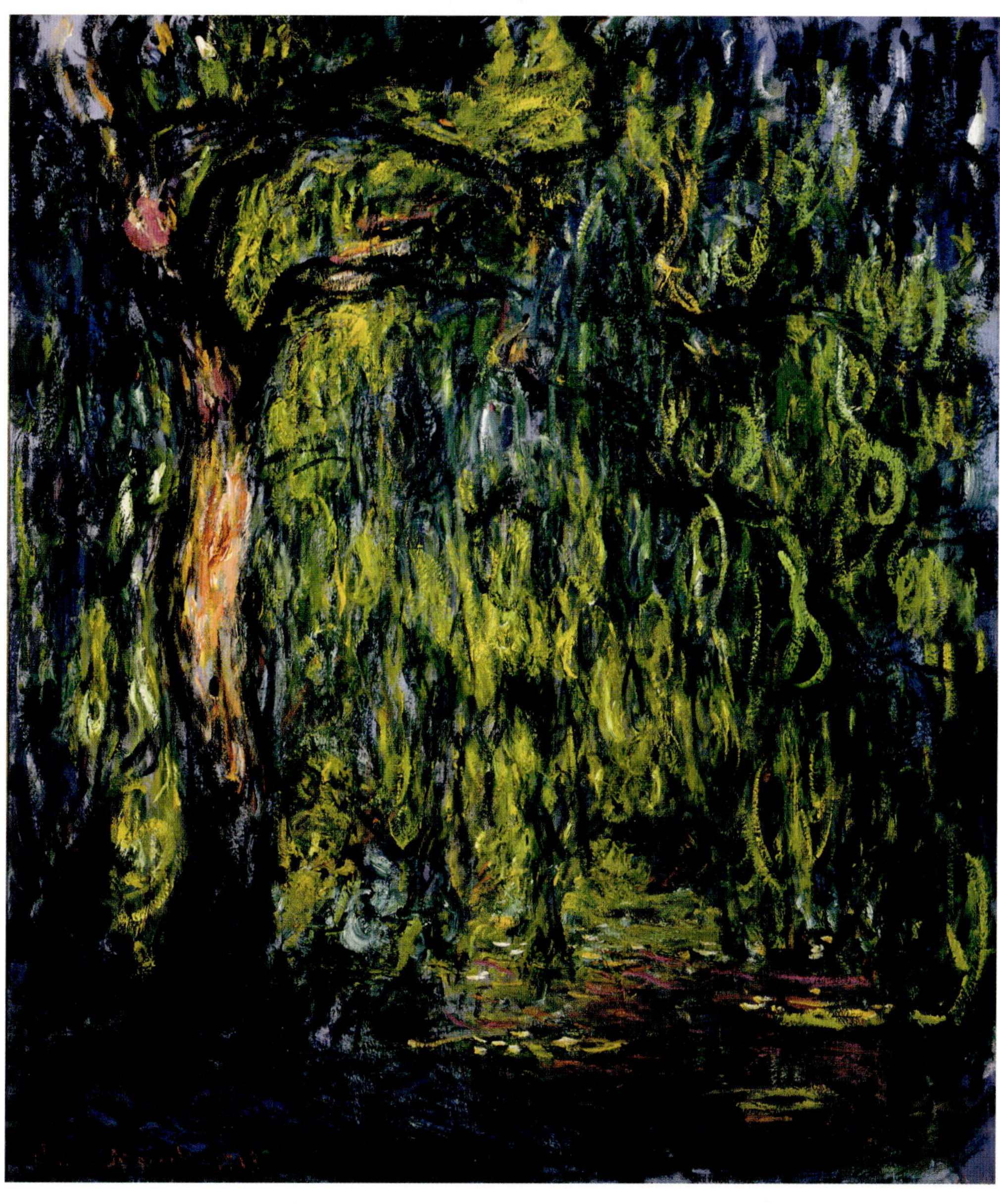

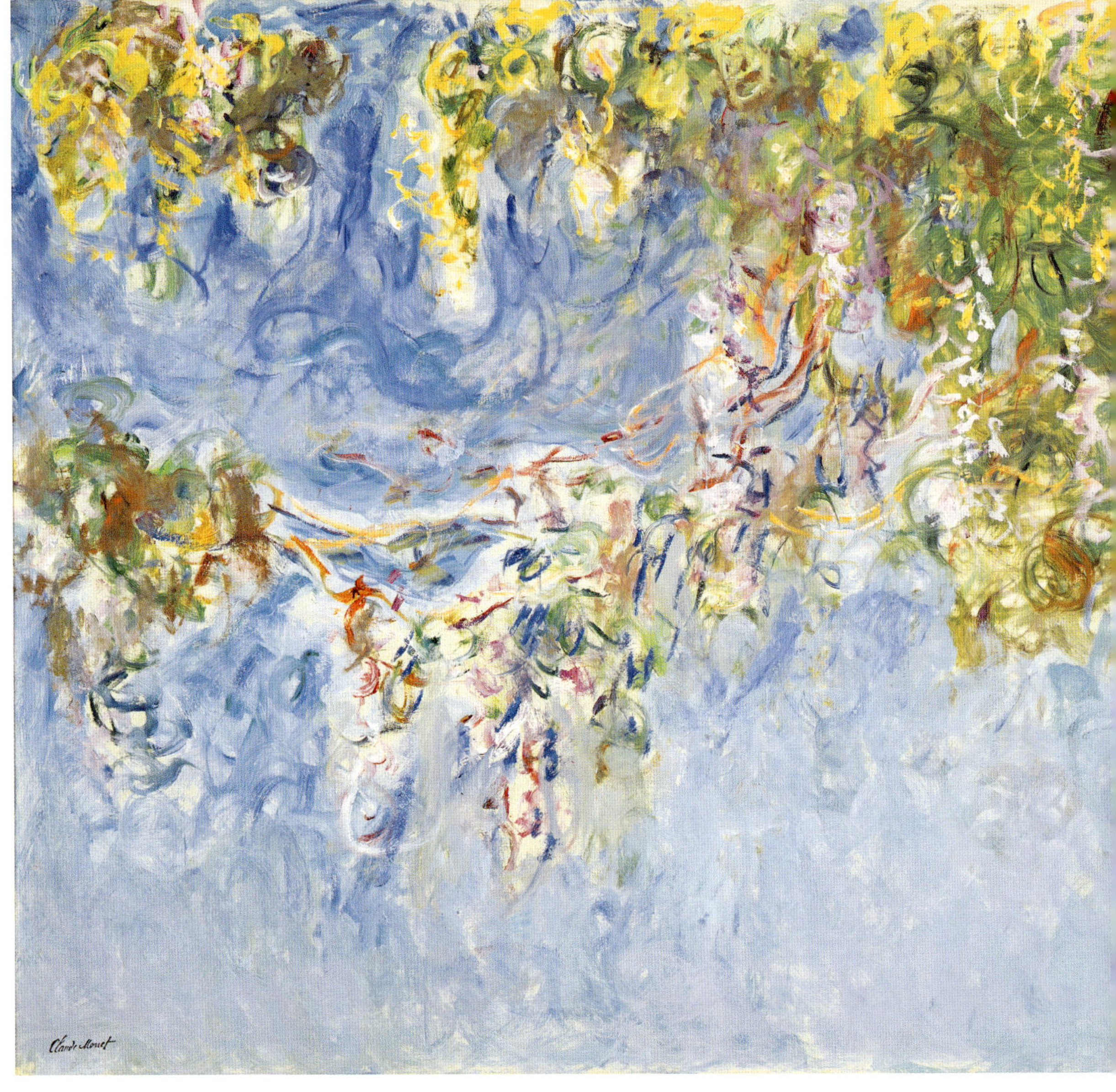
Claude Monet

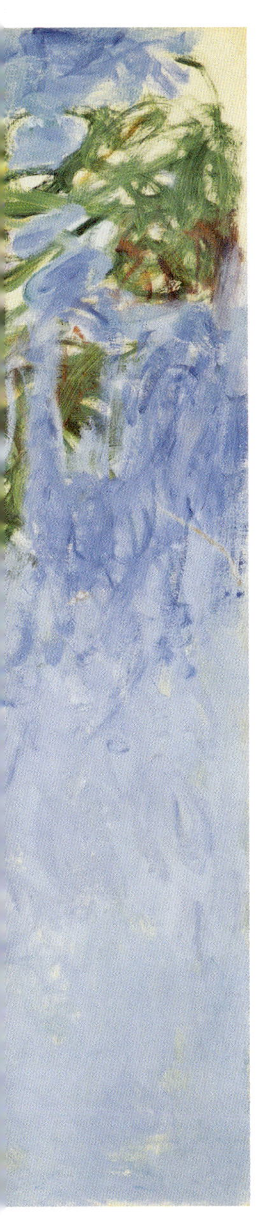

**CAT 11**

*Wisteria (Glycines)*
ca. 1919–20, oil on canvas,
59 × 78 ⅞ in. (149.8 × 200.5 cm)

Allen Memorial Art Museum,
Oberlin College, Oberlin, Ohio:
R.T. Miller Jr. Fund, 1960 (1960.5)

CAT 12

*Wisteria Number 1 and 2*
ca. 1920, oil on canvas,
each panel: 59 × 79 in. (149.9 × 200.7 cm)

Private Collection

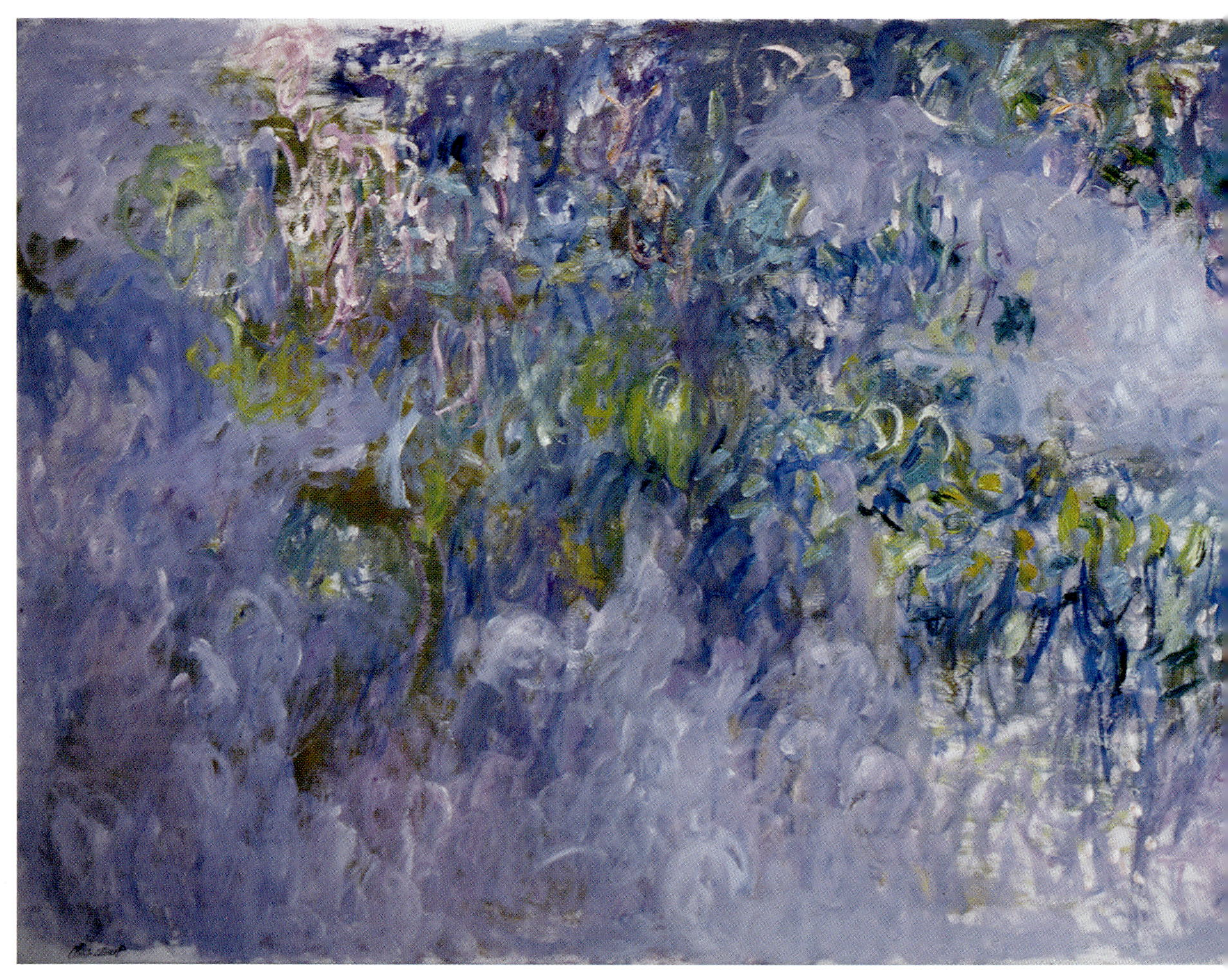

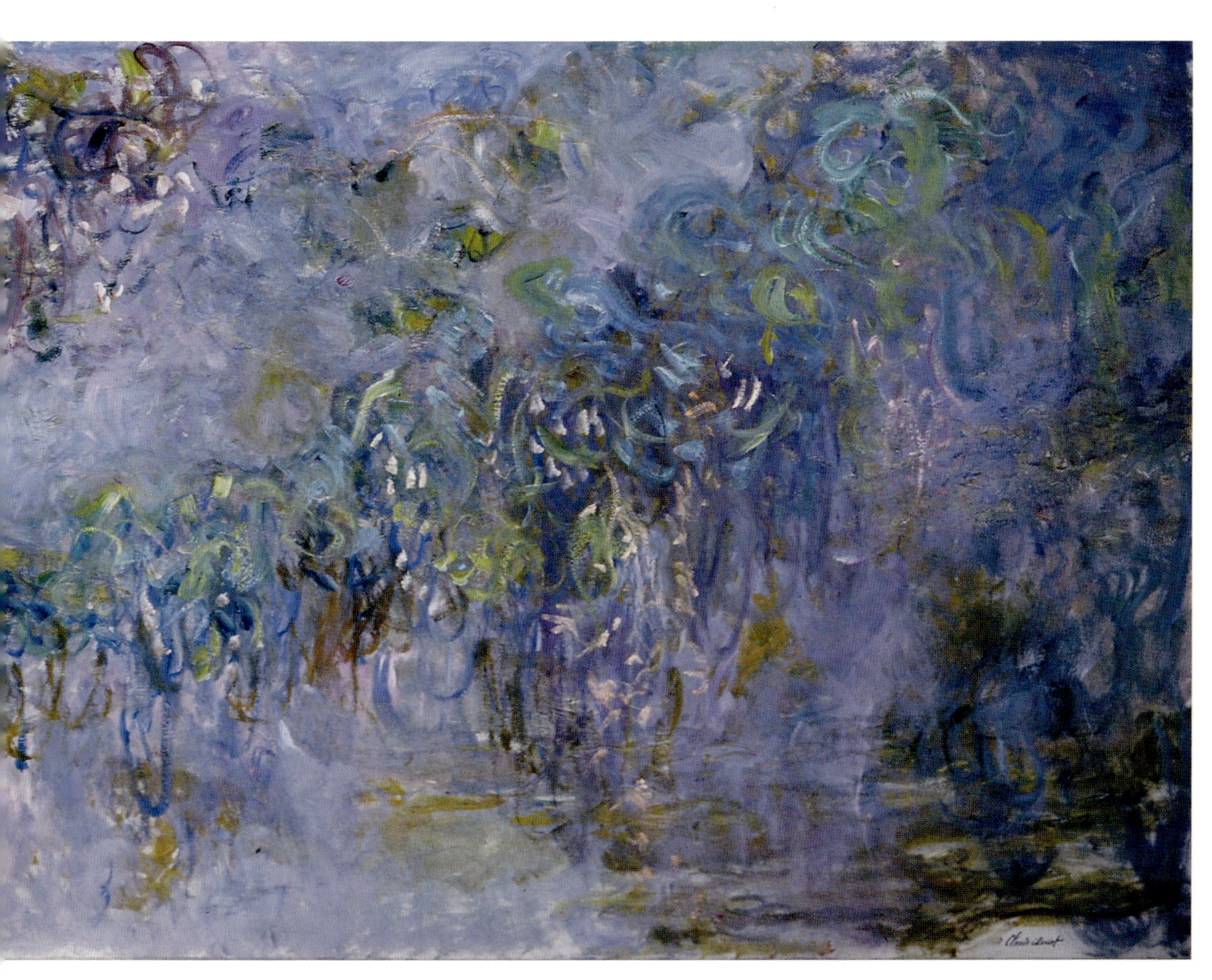

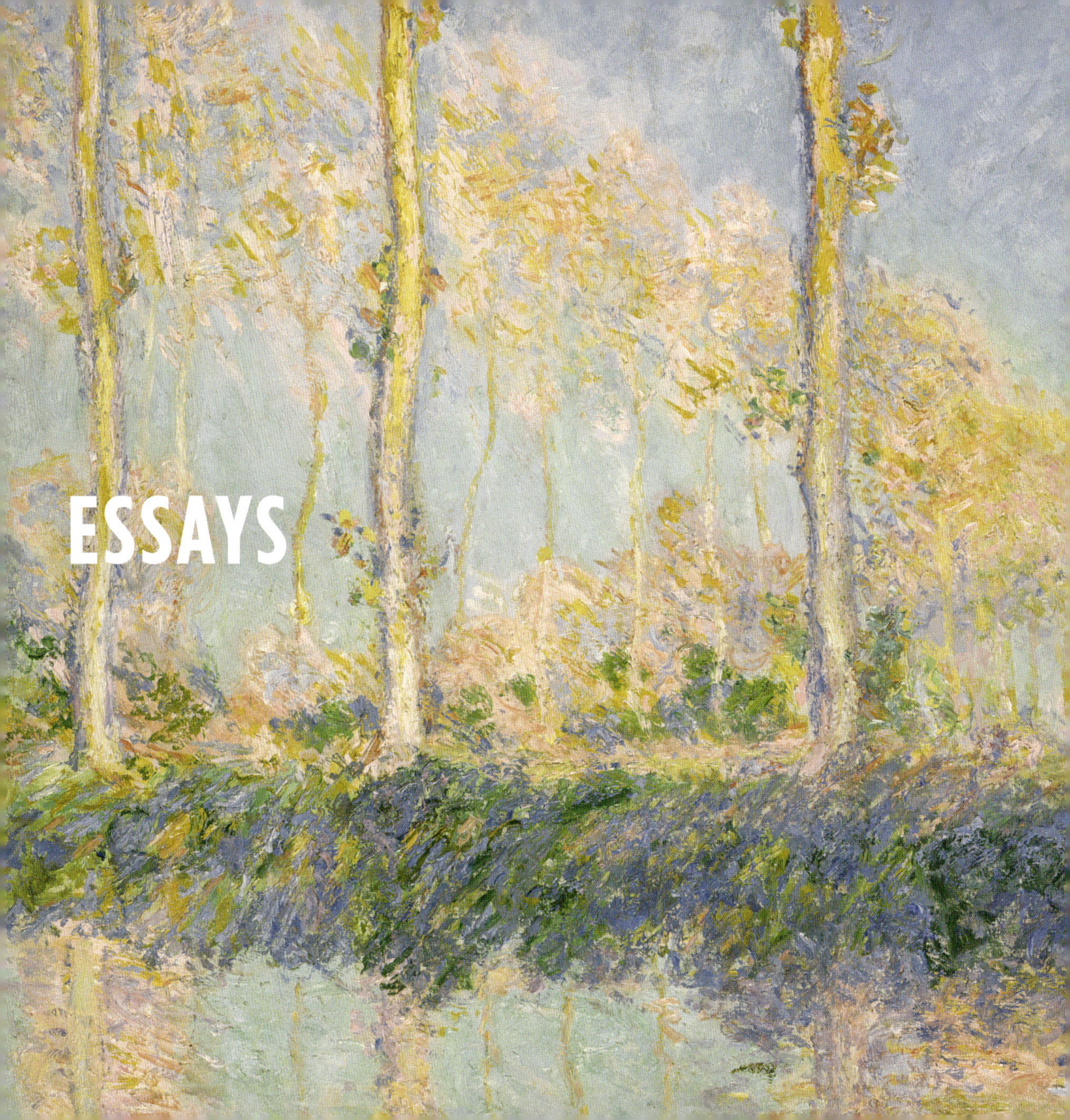

# ESSAYS

## LANDSCAPES, WATERSCAPES, AND REFLECTION IN GIVERNY
*Benedict Leca*

## MIRRORED WATERS
REFLECTIONS ON MONET AND HIS PREDECESSORS
*Lynne D. Ambrosini*

## FRAGMENTS AND REFLECTIONS
MONET, WAR, AND ELLEN JOHNSON
*Andria Derstine*

## FROM INSTANT TO *ENVELOPPE*
REFLECTIONS ON MONET, PHOTOGRAPHY, AND TIME
*Beth E. Wilson*

## MONET AND GIVERNY
*L'ART DANS LES DEUX MONDES* (MARCH 7, 1891)
*Octave Mirbeau*
*Translated by Benedict Leca*

# LANDSCAPES, WATERSCAPES, AND REFLECTION IN GIVERNY

*By Benedict Leca*

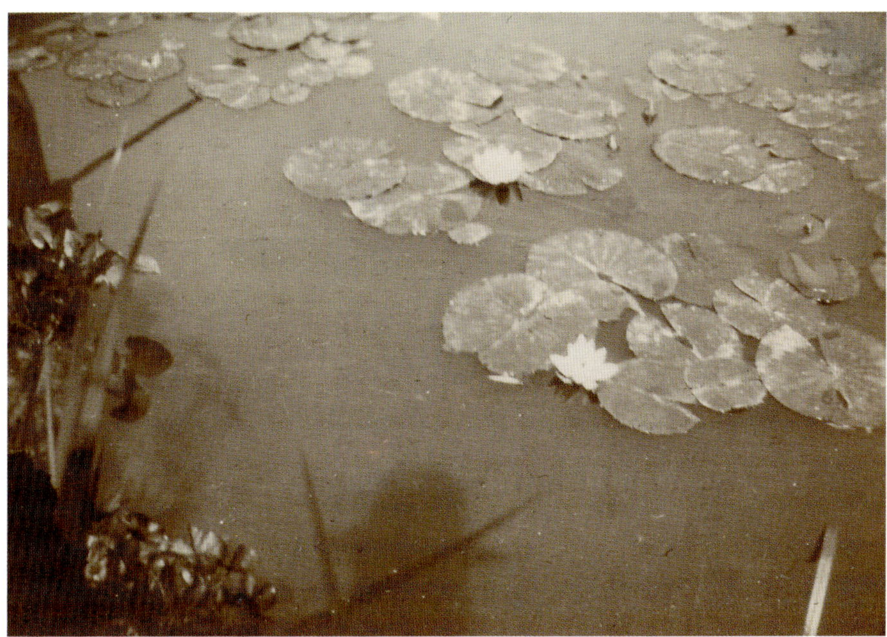

**Fig. 1**
Claude Monet, *Self-Portrait on the Surface of the Water Lily Pond, Giverny*, ca. 1905, salt print from a film negative, 1 11/16 x 2 1/4 in. (4.3 x 5.7 cm), Philippe Piguet Collection

*These landscapes of water and reflections have become my obsession. They are quite beyond the powers of an old man, and despite everything I want to succeed in conveying what I feel.*

Claude Monet to Gustave Geffroy, 1883[1]

*The essence of the motif is the mirror of water whose appearance alters at every moment, thanks to the patches of sky that are reflected in it, and give it its light and movement...*

Claude Monet to François Thiébault-Sisson, 1909[2]

This exhibition takes reflection in all of its meanings as the governing thematic with which we might more fruitfully perceive Monet's late career achievement in Giverny. For indeed, the multiple physical or natural phenomena, states of mind, and symbolic allusions contained in the single term allows for an interpretative narrative of Monet's late work, one that might account for both shifts and continuities in Monet's painting, while remaining grounded in what we know of Monet's own thought process and the historical specificities of his career.[3] Aside from his own statements, as above, the 1886 edition of the Larousse dictionary provides the definitions of reflection and related terms as Monet might have understood them. *Réflexion*: reverberation (reflection of rays); act of the mind that reflects; thoughts that are the product thereof. *Reflet*: reflection of the light of a body's color upon another (reflection of a painting).[4] What is important for us in this lexicographic enumeration is the way that it neatly encompasses the range of meanings of reflection that concerns us here. That is: Monet's preoccupation with capturing water and its reflected light in paint; his and our thinking about his painting; and the experience and effect upon the viewer when looking at his work.

We can be sure that Monet from the very beginning of his career understood reflection critically: his earlier scenes of Impressionist leisure are often defined by shimmering, moving water that is as much a stand-in for the hubbub of modern life as it is the deliberate rendition of natural effects. But whereas his early Impressionism might be characterized roughly as more or less oriented towards observing and capturing the physical occurrence of a reflection, already by the 1870s Monet had shifted to a more contemplative (reflective) practice. The crisp shorthand used to depict fleeting light conditions in earlier works begins to give way to a greater preoccupation with pattern and overall effect, visual impact, and the artifice of painting itself, an affinity that found its first full flowering in the serial paintings of the 1890s. We might think of it as a constantly shifting ratio of attention to naturalism and to artifice, communicated by sometimes comparatively rough paint in contrast to smoothened surface; or by composition and visual orientation; or by illusion and the physical impact on the viewer. The contrasting handling and mood of the exhibited pairing of Seine river scenes near Giverny—*The Seine at Port-Villez* (1883–90) and the *Morning on the Seine, near Giverny* (1896)—(cats. 1 and 3) is a case in point. In spatially divergent compositions, silvery waters transport us to the traditional pendant of storm and calm scenes. Here color and orientation further specify the difference between motion and stillness: in the picture from Columbus, warm, silvery grays and pinks in the picture's foreground define the kinetic energy of glimmering currents, which proffer an accompanying reflection of part of the windswept trees we see on the riverbank perpendicular to us. In the morning scene from Boston, we look downstream from a vantage at the center of the painting upon a scene of cool stillness and a silken paint surface, where the doubled reflection of sky and water obfuscates the horizon line, creating a hazy atmosphere of dissolved forms and stillness amplified by Monet's smoothened paint application.

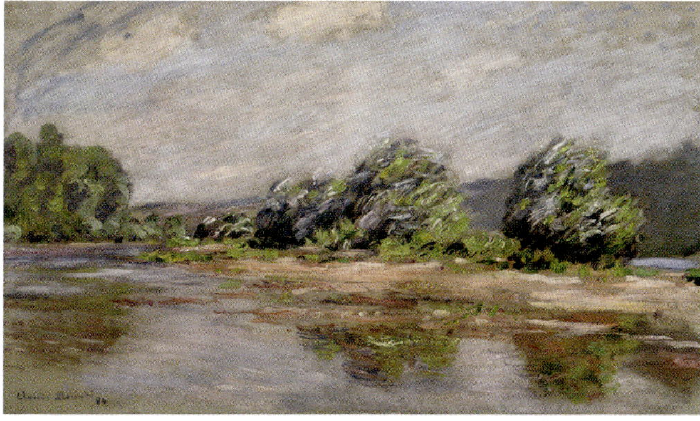

**Cat 1**
*The Seine at Port-Villez (A Gust of Wind) (La Seine à Port-Villez (Le Coup de vent))*
1883–90, oil on canvas,
23 3/4 x 39 1/4 in. (60.3 x 99.7 cm)
Columbus Museum of Art, Ohio: Gift of Howard D. and Babette L. Sirak, the Donors to the Campaign for Enduring Excellence, and the Derby Fund (1991.001.043)

The square format of the *Morning on the Seine* series nonetheless evinces a subsumed geometry that Monet was to adapt to his paintings of the first motif extracted from his personal garden: the Japanese footbridge arching over his lily pond, which he began to paint systematically in the late 1890s. In the pair presented here, separated in date by some two decades, reflective water is an integral element in both compositions, but used to radically different effect (cats. 4 and 5). The earlier *Japanese Footbridge* of the mid-1890s relies on the reflection to further a compositional balance in which the actual bridge coincides directly with its mirrored inverse to arrive at a symmetry that bespeaks rational order. The coloring, too, evokes a landscape pastel of the eighteenth century, making this Japanese footbridge closer in spirit to the earlier poplar series (cat. 2), a series that has been interpreted in terms of a longstanding popular apprehension of patriotic mythologies about the beauty, fertility, and stability of rural France.[5] Compositional balance of this early Japanese bridge, and the commanding rhythm of the poplars morphs in the late picture of the bridge into a reflection reduced in prominence and now applied to an abstracted motif picked out with a variegated touch. The proximity of Monet's position in relation to the motif has led him to crop the bridge and downsize the reflection, yielding a less symmetrical and more abbreviated composition that recalls the elliptical arrangements and graphic charge of Japanese prints. Monet, we know, collected Japanese prints: the cycles of views of Mount Fuji by the master Hokusai or others by Hiroshige were a significant precedent for his serial, ruminative treatment of a single motif.[6] He was also aware of the Japanese conceit of using a fragment to render a whole; just as he effused about meditation. But meditative looking derives here not from the apprehension of glassy, serene water, but from a rough, dynamic paint layer and a pronounced decorative patterning that invites close contemplation of the facture as much as the depiction. One might in this light venture a step further in seeing Monet's impastoed paint in philosophical terms of materiality, where water would have here mixed with earth to yield a primordial paste that, according to the philosopher Gaston Bachelard, we should understand to be the "the basic component of materiality."[7]

> "The Garden is the man."
> Arsène Alexandre, 1901[8]

Monet wasn't just obsessed with reflection, but also with self-reflection, or a methodological awareness of his craft that was explicit in mirrored surfaces—the basis of the reflected face of self-portraiture. With his self-expressive practice founded on his insistent engagement with the depiction of water and its chromatic effects, Monet went on learning ever more about his own feelings before watery motifs and how best to convey them. It is an aesthetic journey of self-discovery that can be tracked geographically: his first arrival in Giverny in 1883 was in fact the penultimate stage in a trajectory that saw Monet address watery subjects in systematically more distant locales northwest of Paris until his last retreat to the boundaries of his innermost garden. In this way Monet lived the chestnut of contemporary travel literature that would have the journey outward, the movement away from the metropolis, become a stand-in for the journey inward.

It is helpful here to consider time elapsed, the time of active travel and its conventional difference from that required for the autobiographical recounting of the incidents of travel afterwards. Monet initially sought to conflate the two, a conflation he lived in real terms, despite his later disavowal. He discusses the issues in the oft-cited discussion with the critic Thiébault-Sisson, where he admits to having originally wanted to attempt in each painting "a sort of synthesis in which I would sum up...my past impressions and sensations."[9] Thus Giverny's bucolic charms specifically enabled Monet to enact as well as recount his expressive journey by means of his garden design and painting—to create an idyll where he could reflect on his practice while imaging himself and his evolving aesthetic through his increasing focus on specific garden motifs, notably his water lily paintings. The exhibition brings together four exceptional water lily paintings of differing formats (cats. 6–9), three from Monet's initial campaign of 1903–9 and a late work dating to 1916–19, which together testify first to the variety as well as complexity of effects achieved by the artist in his series of water lily paintings. Monet himself was explicit in communicating the crux of his treatment of his signature motif: "The essence of the motif (water lily) is the mirror of water whose appearance alters at every moment."[10] And so his repeated treatment of the reflective surfaces of his pond and the kaleidoscopic color variations of its flora visible above and beneath mirrored water served as an interminable canvas, where both motif and metaphor of reflection combined directly in the service of self-definition. In the water lilies from Dayton (cat. 6), for example, a refractive, silvery water surface mirrors a sky of shifting clouds, as it intimates a receding spatial illusion punctuated by wisteria leaves emphatically daubed on the picture surface at the upper left, there to remind us of the material flatness of the canvas and, not least, of the artist's presence.

Monet's sheer output of water lily canvases—some 250 over the course of nearly twenty-five years—effectively demands an analogy between the infinity of nature and the breadth of our painter's imagination. And it is no surprise to find that his water lily paintings were first critiqued in just such terms when, in May 1909, at his dealer Durand-Ruel's gallery, Monet first presented an astounding suite of forty-eight of his self-described "waterscapes" (*Nymphéas*). The critic Arsène Alexandre, reviewing the exhibition, verbalizes a tripartite conflation of the artist's imagination, nature, and the bounty of an expanded, mirrored world reproduced ad infinitum:

> ...these paintings [have] no other beginnings or ends than the limits of the frame, which imagination can extend to wherever it pleases. The sole elements [comprising] these paintings is an aquatic mirror, the flowers and leaves that rest upon it, and then the reflection of the surrounding landscape, diffuse and of infinite variety...in a marvelous and capricious diversity."[11]

This gushing, overheated rhetoric before Monet's refractive confections was in many ways conventional criticism, or rather an example of the particular genre of near ekphrastic description whose exponents sought verbal equivalents for the visual pyrotechnics of Monet's brush. One is hard-pressed, for example, in reading the writer and critic Octave Mirbeau's essay on the master in Giverny translated in this volume, to disentangle which, between Monet's garden and Monet's paintings, enchanted the author more. Mirbeau limns a world as well as an artistic career in it, in a sustained flight of poetic art criticism by one of the great contemporary champions of Monet and his art. His text is notable for its mystical inflections and hagiographic emphases, with Monet fulfilling a cosmographic destiny: Monet is the creator of "this passionate, moving, fluid nature, where, among the tender sensualities, lies the dream, there at every step, which seizes and draws one towards the mysterious, profound, and always novel celebration of the hours."[12]

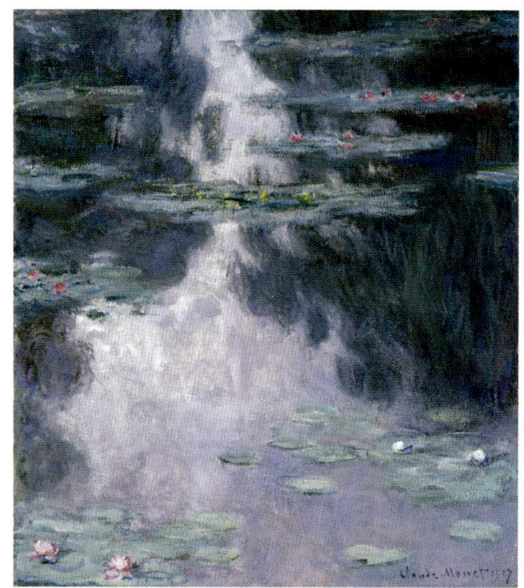

**Cat. 8**
Claude Monet, *Water Lilies (Nymphéas)*, 1907, oil on canvas, 36 1/4 x 31 15/16 in. (92.1 x 81.2 cm), The Museum of Fine Arts, Houston: Gift of Mrs. Harry C. Hanszen (68.31)

It is in Mirbeau's more pointedly descriptive passages that we can perhaps find a more accessible coincidence between text and image, and indeed his description of Monet's ineffable rendering of aquatic flora visible through the shifting river waters deploys a bedazzled naturalist's eye that gestures to the holistic forces contained in nature. We might perceive this will to transcendence in formal terms in the Denver and Houston water lilies (cats. 7 and 8) in the way that we are presented with a world fully in the round—that we apprehend from every direction. Both pictures give a complex of reflections of sky, of water surface, of submerged flora, and a spatial arrangement that is both recessive as illusion and material on canvas projecting forward into our space. The Denver picture gives greater emphasis to the rendering of submerged forms as an "all-over" effect, whereas the Houston painting yields an equilibrium between effects of sky and water, shown visually as the balanced patterning of two equal areas of contrasting light and dark on the canvas. Speaking of an infinity when looking into the proverbial abyss, the Houston canvas gives us a simultaneous view into the infinite stratospheric reaches of the sky reflected in the water surface and a view, in the picture's upper right quadrant, into the somewhat menacing shadows of a bottomless aquatic world. For Mirbeau and some of his contemporaries there existed a brooding, romantic aspect to Monet's otherworldly scenes, one strangely discordant with the prevailing view of Monet's art today as all sunshine and flowers.

> ...[Through] the mirrored, brilliant surface of flowing water, the eye penetrates little by little into this wavy freshness...and discovers there through this liquid clarity an entire life of lake flora, an extraordinary submerged vegetation of

long, stringy wild weeds of greenish purple, which, in the flow of the current, flutter, twist, dangle, spread out and gather up like soft bizarre hairs; then undulate, waver, turn around and extend forth like strange fish, like the fantastic tentacles of marine monsters.[13]

Mirbeau is here essentially describing the effect given in the upper right half of the 1907 water lilies from Houston, where we peer into the striated world of "stringy wild weeds of greenish purple." At the center of the canvas, where the two elements meet, Monet pictures the distinctions and analogies between air and water, which are set alongside each other and twinned visually in the coagulating weave of the paint surface. Yet what was significant in tone and theme to Mirbeau seriously implicates issues particular to painting and representation, notably in the way that Monet mobilizes the reflection as opaque mirror and translucent lens to image a dialogue between spatial illusion and the materiality of surfaces, inciting in turn our own dialogic grapplings as viewers with these same issues. The directed prominence of the reflection, which dominates the bottom half of the canvas, structures the scene vertically, leading one's eye back in space that has been tilted forward. The effect is further glossed by the artist through his handling of paint; the pasty materiality of Monet's rich paint layer in parts of the upper half of the canvas, notably the reflection and the additive impasto used to render the water lilies and their bloom, signals a disavowal of traditional aerial perspective. Where aerial perspective is conventionally achieved using effaced brushwork and faded, blue tonalities to denote the haze enveloping distant reflections, Monet insists on recalcitrant notes of emphatic impasto or conspicuous color that self-consciously flaunt his touch as enabling and disarming spatial illusionism.

## REFLECTION AND THE EXPANDED FIELD OF PAINTING

This last point regarding the relationship between depicted depth and two-dimensional flatness is an important one that positions Monet's self-definition in paint within the continuum of modernist, avant-garde painting. Here reflection, or the depiction thereof, makes clear the analogy between reflected images and painted images, and in turn implicates us as self-conscious viewers whose perception before the painted mirror is joined to the artist's apprehension of his watery motif. The conflation of our perception with that of the painter's through our viewing of his paintings is made explicit in the water lilies from an important Midwest private collection (cat. 9), where the closely cropped viewpoint onto lily pads devoid of any spatial indices mimics our field of vision. Monet began painting water lilies as close-up studies before expanding his purview. Nonetheless, he steadily evolves towards a tighter focus on larger, isolated flowers in his later iterations, pictures which often position the viewer as floating above the water lilies precisely like Monet himself in the opening photograph of his shadow reflected on the water surface (fig. 1). Paintings, of course, hang vertically, and so we can spy Monet here engaging in a sort of musing on the ready associations of a painting as mirror, which would refute or inflect the recessive space of traditional perspective. This oppositional maneuver is literalized in the shadow portrait of the opening photograph (fig. 1), and realized in paint to culminating effect in the late oversize canvases of wisterias shown in the present exhibition.

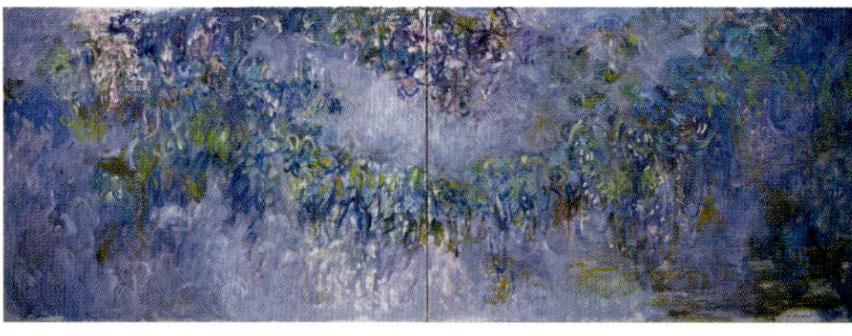

**Cat. 12**
Claude Monet, *Wisteria Number 1 and 2*, ca. 1920, oil on canvas, each panel: 59 x 79 in. (149.9 x 200.7 cm), Private Collection

Listed in Wildenstein's catalogue raisonné of Monet's paintings consecutively, the combined three panels of wisterias, which have an aggregate length of some twenty-one feet, were created during the same period (cats. 11 and 12); and we might venture that they are together in the present exhibition for the first time since ca. 1920 when they could have coexisted in Monet's studio. This chronological connection would in fact be of a piece with the viewing impact that Monet sought with his *Grandes Décorations*, the enormous water lily paintings of his late career that were in full production by 1919. Even if the panel from Oberlin (cat. 11) was never exhibited in Monet's lifetime, its formal conception is in large part intended to produce a desired transportative effect, where an amorphous spatiality intermittently appears as a set of surrounding mirrors that refract into infinity. To position Monet's achievement in relation to the work of another groundbreaking artist such as Paul Cézanne provides perspective on the lineage that valorized structure and geometry over Monet's organic pattern. Cézanne's talismanic view of Lake Annecy at the Courtauld Gallery (fig. 2) underscores the geometry of structure, in a picture dominated by rectilinear effects. Structure suggests stasis, while when we speak of Cézanne we are dealing with one of the foundational masters at confounding restrictions of space. No question that Cézanne achieves a dynamic, and fluctuating, balance between depth and flatness: his picture does indeed "breathe," to reprise a famous formulation.[14] But for all of the blue water and shifting effects, Cézanne proves

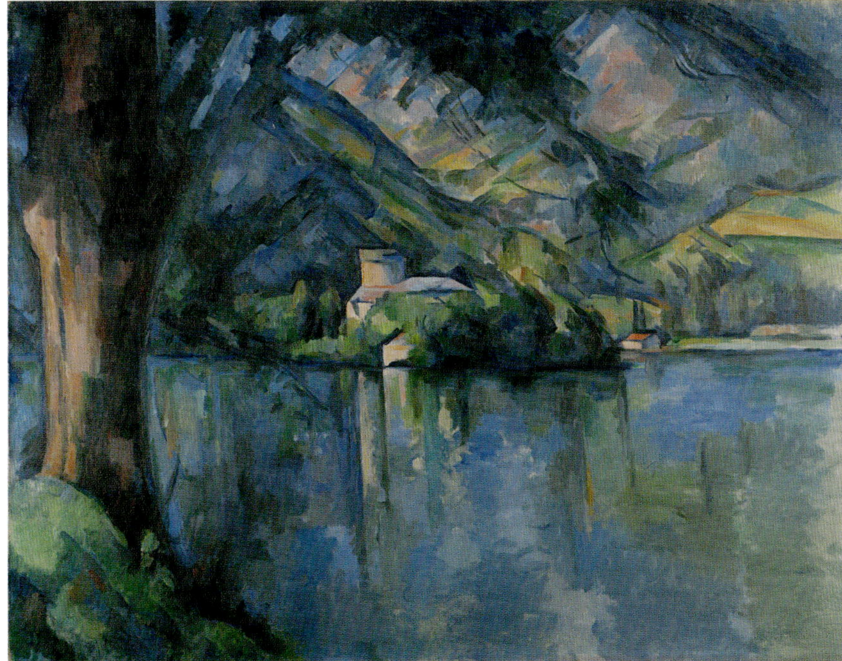

**Fig. 2**
Paul Cézanne, *The Lac d'Annecy*, 1896, oil on canvas, 25 9/16 x 31 7/8 in. (65 x 81 cm), Courtauld Institute of Art Gallery, The Samuel Courtauld Trust (P.1932.SC.60)

here that his aesthetic should always remain linked to the dry, telluride geometry of Cubism rather than to the fluid waterscapes of Monet's Giverny.[15] It is in this light that we can rationalize the marginalization of Monet's counter-current enterprise for much of the first half of the twentieth century, as if water and flowers couldn't possibly address the bases of modernist representation or the machine age. But in fact Monet broke the mirror that for all times subtended traditional perspective, invoking the cinematographic, for one, in the astounding lengths of canvas he devoted to large decorative painting in his last years. Wall cycles of paintings foretold in this way the immersive video production of today's contemporary art. And indeed the wisteria panels shown in the present exhibition create a reflective, surrounding atmosphere that conflates sky and water, one which confounds traditional spatial illusion as it envelops our physical space as viewers, an effect we might compare in a final instance to the breaching or breaking of the surface mirror through which we are plunged into vaporous water.

# MIRRORED WATERS

## REFLECTIONS ON MONET AND HIS PREDECESSORS

*By Lynne D. Ambrosini*

*"The reflected world is the conquest of calm."*

Gaston Bachelard, *Water and Dreams*, 1942[1]

Consider the difficulties of depicting water: its liquidity, which allows formless expansion; its edgeless clarity, which defies drawing; and its reflective properties, which make it ever-changing. The problem of how to render it remained minor, however, until the nineteenth century, when landscape came to dominate the art market and demands for realism increased. Then the issue of how to paint water, and especially *reflecting* water, challenged leading landscapists from Pierre-Henri Valenciennes through the Impressionists. It stimulated new pictorial solutions from Camille Corot, Charles-François Daubigny, and Gustave Courbet—all of whose work Monet admired—and of course from Monet himself. In about 1896, he began painting the pond in his Giverny garden and continued for some thirty years, explaining that his true subject was "the mirror of water whose appearance alters at every moment."[2] Situating Monet's practices in relation to those of his predecessors, I will explore how each conceived landscapes with aqueous reflections, what significances lay latent in them, and what Monet may have learned from each.

Mid-nineteenth-century French landscape emerged from the matrix of Neo-Classical landscape, which had actually codified rules for painting reflections in water. In fact, an unusually stable praxis of landscape painting existed between the revolutions of 1789 and 1830. It owed much to the talents of the period's greatest landscapist and erudite champion of the genre, Pierre-Henri de Valenciennes (1750–1819). He taught at the École des Beaux-Arts in Paris (from 1812), and wrote the movement's bible, *Élémens de perspective pratique à l'usage des artistes.*[3] With editions in 1800 and 1820, the text guided two generations of aspiring French landscapists. Valenciennes trained them to present convincing illusions of a perfected nature, enlivened with narratives from the ancient authors, for the pleasure and moral edification of wealthy, well-educated patrons. Both of Corot's teachers, Jean-Victor Bertin and Achille-Etna Michallon, studied with him.

Valenciennes devoted three sections of *Élémens de perspective* to the topic of accurately limning reflections in water.[4] Most critical were three pages of geometric instruction that required a compass and ruler: "Continue to draw the perpendicular (D-E) below the line

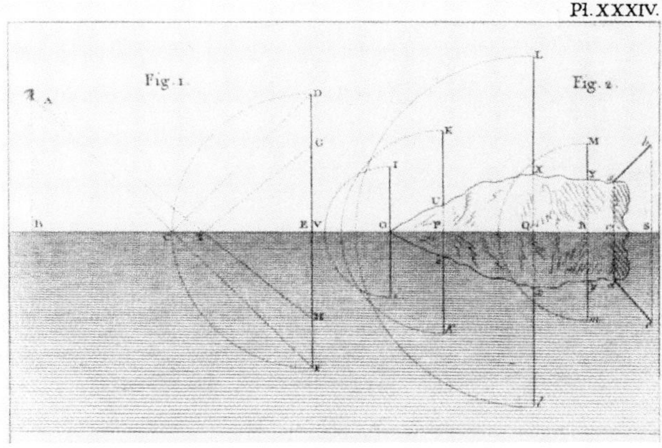


**Fig. 3**
Pierre-Henri de Valenciennes, *Diagram of perspective for reflections of objects in water*, from *Élémens de perspective pratique à l'usage des artistes* (Paris: Aimé Payen, 1820, second edition), plate XXXIV

(B-E)…"[5] Supplementing the text, diagrams illustrated the constructions (fig. 3). Valenciennes based his method on René Descartes's well-known optical law of reflection.[6] He dealt mainly with still water, for his exacting reflections could appear only there. Valenciennes also noted that the color of each reflection should be lighter than the color of its corresponding object.

A canvas by François-Xavier Fabre, *The Death of Narcissus* (1814), demonstrates the application of Valenciennes's methods.[7] It tells the cautionary story from Ovid in which water served as mirror to the youth Narcissus. Enchanted with his own reflection, Narcissus perished while admiring it.[8] We know that Fabre followed Valenciennes's treatise to the letter:[9] Narcissus, a goddess, a maiden, a dog, and a funerary monument reflect precisely in the pool's glassy waters.

As a foil for later nineteenth-century interpretations, what matters about Neo-Classical landscapes is the underlying Enlightenment assumption that mathematics can map out reflections for painters. Such landscapes each have a single, fixed viewpoint imposed by the perspective scheme. To create them, an artist located each landscape element and its proportionate reflection in the drawn spatial grid, and only then picked up the brush. Thus each painted reflection constitutes a simulacrum of its referent object. In this conception of landscape, reflections signify observable phenomena, susceptible of being plumbed by science, in a rational universe.

Fortunately, Jean-Baptiste-Camille Corot (1796–1875) paid more heed to Valenciennes's exhortations to sketch in oil outdoors than he did to the master's geometry.[10] In an early Italian canvas, *Lake Piediluco* (1826), Corot sought just the right tones (from light to dark) and the perfect greens and blues to evoke the soft, reflecting light of morning on the lake.[11] He depended little on the preparatory drawings Valenciennes recommended, but relied instead on direct observation, sketching his subject only summarily in pencil first, and then proceeding to painting.[12] In *Lake Piediluco,* the cool reflections have flat, non-perspectival shapes and are—by Valenciennes's standards—fudged.

Similarly, the light-suffused reflections in Corot's *Lake Nemi, Seen through Trees* (1843) are all about color and tonal gradation, not line.[13] The misty hills at the edge of the famed lake near Rome, known as the "mirror of Diana," reflect in the lake in delicately modulated, tinted tones. In transcribing his immediate perceptions into paint, Corot opened the door to Impressionism.

In a painting that Monet undoubtedly saw at the Salon of 1864, *Memory of Mortefontaine*, Corot produced his most famous reflecting composition (fig. 4).[14]

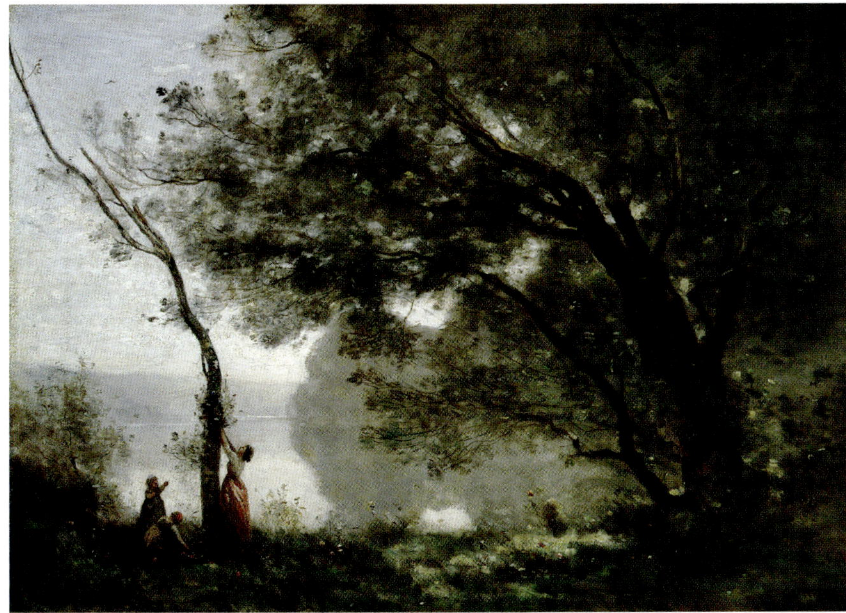

**Fig. 4**
Jean-Baptiste-Camille Corot, *Memory of Mortefontaine, France (Souvenir de Mortefontaine)*, 1864, oil on canvas, 25 5/8 x 35 in. (65 x 89 cm), Louvre, Paris, France (M.I. 692 bis)

Again he selected a lake vista, seen under *contre-jour* light that casts shadowy reflections of the distant trees upon the water. As before, Corot shaped the scene into a tripartite planar composition, arranging the foreground, reflecting waters, and distant shore in ranks parallel to the picture surface. As a series of *coulisses,* the layout conveniently lacked receding elements, so he could dispense with linear perspective. Instead, Corot created distance through inflections of touch and color: a carefully graduated hierarchy of stroke-size and impastos mimic the visual experience of nearer things being brighter and bolder, and distant things being blue-ish and smoother. No longer structured by contour and grid, such compositions helped form Monet and his peers.[15]

A generation younger than Corot, Charles-François Daubigny (1817–1878) arguably exerted an even greater influence on Monet in the development of the reflecting waterscape. In the fall of 1857, he invented the floating atelier to paint vistas of the Seine directly from midstream.[16] Then in paintings such as *The Village of Gloton* (1857), Daubigny explored the new vantage points the boat afforded (fig. 5). Working in the tranquil waterway between the riverbanks and an island, he

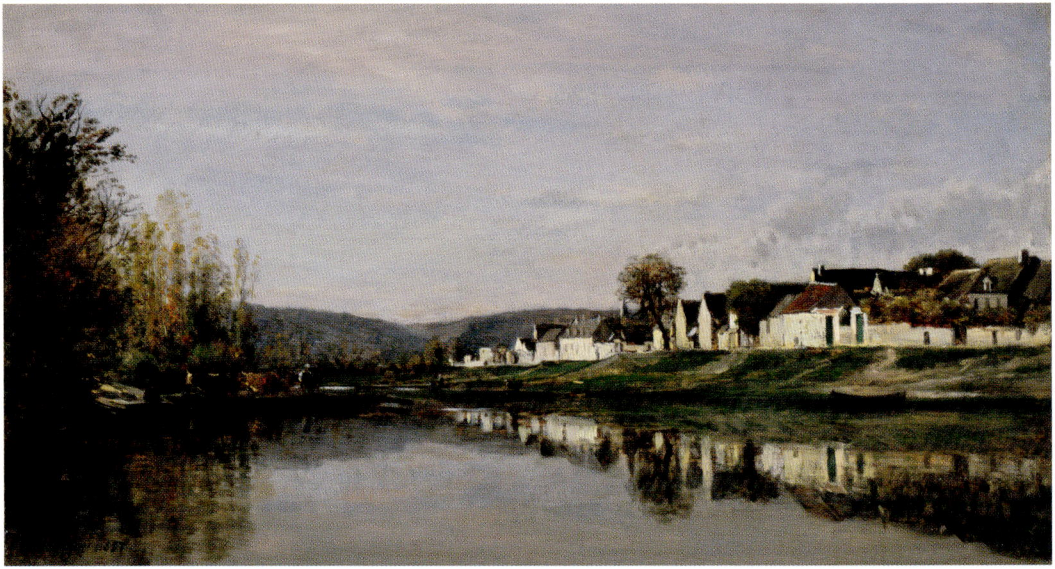

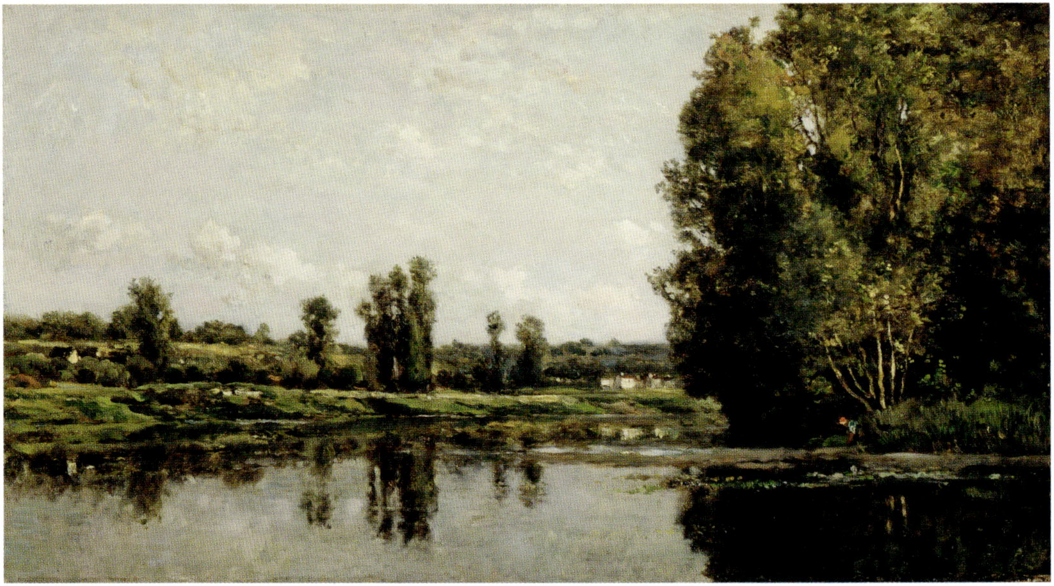

brushed this small panel all at once, working wet into wet,[17] to capture the autumnal scene directly. Like Corot, Daubigny built space by means of zones: the river, the land (in this case seen obliquely), and the distant hills. Stripped of conventional terrestrial foregrounds, fresh in color, and acutely observed, these views astonished his contemporaries. His compositions gave pride of place to reflective passages, in which he used chastened hues and intensities for the mirrored portions to subordinate them to the houses above.

Daubigny first exhibited his midstream river subjects at the Salon of 1859. The young Monet admired his submissions, writing to Eugène Boudin: "To me, the Daubignys are really something beautiful."[18] In many subsequent painting campaigns of the 1860s and 70s, Daubigny traveled and worked from his boat to portray the distinctive atmosphere and reflections of a specific prospect at a given time of day. In *On the Banks of the Oise* (1866), trees in the middle ground block the late afternoon sun, whose golden light pervades the peaceful scene (fig. 6). Daubigny used multiple glazes, tinctured with dilute pigments, to evoke the moist summer air.[19] Muted reflections echo the shoreline trees; each has a faint, watery double.

Daubigny, like Corot, represented reflections empirically: intuitive experiments replaced theory. Whereas Corot continued to produce occasional historical landscapes into the decade of the 1860s, however, Daubigny painted his last in 1840. France had changed. Artists had to pander to a new, more middle-class audience, which could also consume their creations through reproductive engravings or commentary from a burgeoning cultural press. What did such spectators appreciate in the two painters' hushed views? Beyond the picturesque beauties of pure landscape—free of any troublingly recondite references—the mirror-like reflection symbolized serenity, the (supposedly) unchanging nature of the rivers at the heart of France.[20] Quite literally, their images showed a world standing still. Seeking out untroubled river inlets or lakes, and avoiding factories, steamboats, and freight barges, Corot and Daubigny summoned a comforting memory of the old rural France before the Industrial Revolution.

In 1872, Monet built his own studio boat to depict the Seine at Argenteuil.[21] Daubigny was then still plying the waters of the Oise and Seine and the two painters were friendly.[22] Many of Monet's mid-river views at Argenteuil of 1872–74, with their shimmering reflections, implicitly acknowledged the older painter, although Monet enlarged and broke up the strokes that captured the reflections.[23]

**Fig. 5**
Charles-François Daubigny, *The Village of Gloton,* 1857, oil on panel, 11 3/4 x 21 1/2 in. (29.8 x 53.7 cm), Fine Arts Museums of San Francisco, Mildred Anna Williams Collection (1940.4)

**Fig. 6**
Charles-François Daubigny, *On the Banks of the Oise,* 1866, oil on panel, 14 1/2 x 26 in. (37.5 x 66.4 cm), The Montreal Museum of Fine Arts, Mrs. W.W. Chipman Bequest (1950.1032)

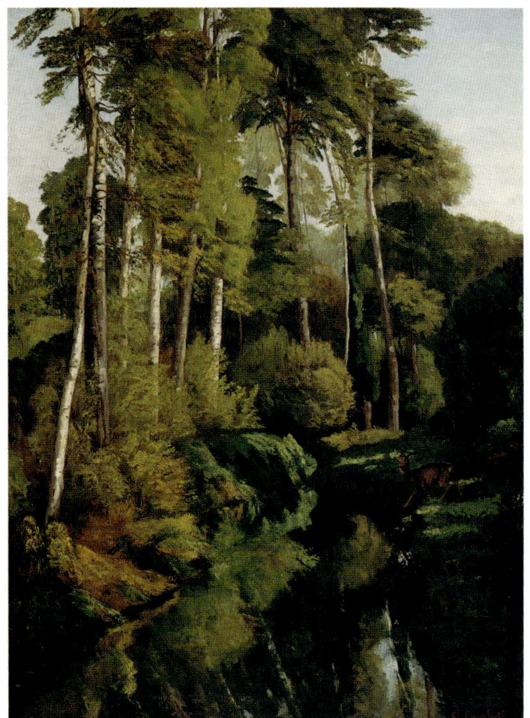

**Fig. 7**
Gustave Courbet, *Stream in the Forest*, ca. 1862, oil on canvas, 61 x 44 7/8 in. (156.8 x 114 cm), Museum of Fine Arts, Boston, Gift of Mrs. Samuel Parkman Oliver (55.982)

In this exhibition, Monet's later *The Seine at Port-Villez*, 1883–90 (cat. 1), though handled more broadly, harks back to Daubigny's waterway pictures.

A third great landscapist in the 1860s, Gustave Courbet, also depicted the still waters of rivers and pools. In the *Stream in the Forest* (ca. 1862), Courbet found his subject in a quiet brook with elms reflecting in the water (fig. 7).[24] This image carries the same connotations that I have suggested for Corot's and Daubigny's work: modern urban spectators could dream of escaping into the harmonious scene. Yet the lowest zone of the picture contains surprises: Courbet broke one of Valenciennes's rules by letting the bright reflected note of turquoise equal the brilliance of the sky above. Further, his rough palette knife application endows the reflections with an unusual independence, calling attention to his process.

In many renditions of the Puits Noir, a forest pool near Courbet's native Ornans, he repeatedly painted still waters. From the first of these, in 1855, through the later versions from the 1860s, his approach was experimental—more material and various than that of any earlier painter. He used great wide brushes, scumbled thick pigments across the canvas, and scraped them with a knife.[25] In a motionless version of the subject about 1860–65,[26] boulders and aged trees cast dark reflections in the pool. Yet even such quieter variants of Courbet's *Puits Noir* astounded observers because their vigorous surfaces ruptured the very illusions of reflectivity that the painting purportedly conveyed.

Monet and Courbet spent time together in the 1860s.[27] Though unlike Courbet in temperament and painting style, Monet undoubtedly studied the older painter's audacious landscapes.[28] I am not suggesting a specific connection between Courbet's forest pools and Monet's Giverny pictures, but the older painter did model relevant practices: his notable freedom of painterly means; fixation on a quiet pool, seen at close range; and sacrifice of pictorial illusions to surface activity.

One painting of riparian reflections by the young Monet seems best to summarize his debt to earlier painters and to anticipate certain aspects of the

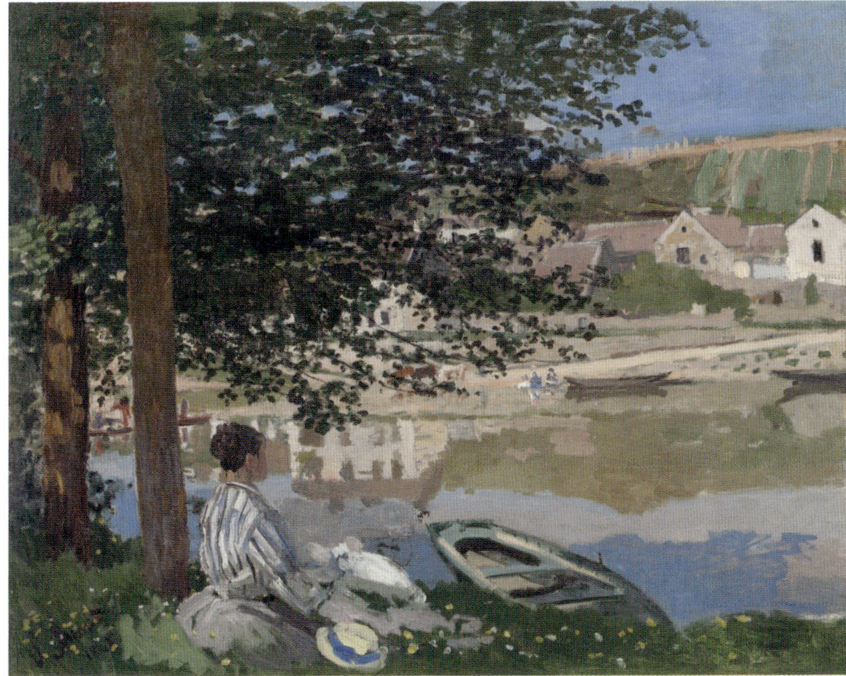

**Fig. 8**
Claude Monet, *On the Bank of the Seine, Bennecourt*, 1868, oil on canvas, 32 1/16 x 39 5/8 in. (81.5 x 100.7 cm), The Art Institute of Chicago, Potter Palmer Collection (1922.427)

Giverny pictures. In *On the Bank of the Seine, Bennecourt* (1868) (fig. 8), Monet painted the very motif that Daubigny had first selected in 1857 (fig. 5) and repeated in several later pictures.[29] It dates from the spring of 1868, when Monet stayed in the hamlet Daubigny had painted, Gloton, on the outskirts of Bennecourt.[30] He had his future wife, Camille, pose on the island that appears to the left in Daubigny's picture. While she gazes at the village, its mirrored image floats on the river. As in the work of Corot and Daubigny, here the still, reflecting water suggests a mood of quiet reverie, reinforced by the meditative figure.

Monet's vantage point behind Camille implies a single viewpoint, yet he, like Corot and Daubigny (figs. 4 and 6), disregarded conventional perspective, borrowing their planar scheme to establish pictorial space. Dissimilarly, though, Monet violated two centuries of landscape decorum by abjuring the time-honored graduated scale and relief of brushstrokes to suggest distance. We might well detect Courbet's example in this. Monet employed sketchy brushwork and large flat dabs of paint even for the distant village, and brushed on the mid-ground reflections with larger strokes than he used for the foreground. As we look, Valenciennes's space—even Daubigny's space—collapses, leaving flatness, while the reflections take on their own life.

Moreover, in the Bennecourt canvas the reflections give information about the site that we, the viewers, cannot actually see: the clouds in the sky, for example, and images of houses fronting the Seine that tree branches block from us. Resulting from a purely optical approach to the subject, this novel device anticipates Monet's *Water Lilies*—the Houston picture for example (cat. 8)—in which the shadowy reflections of unseen trees fall on the water. In this respect Monet parted company with earlier French landscapists, whose objects always appeared twinned with their reflections.[31]

Such motionless waters appear only rarely in Monet's early and mid-career work.[32] Most of his watery subjects of the later 1860, 70s, and 80s, from La Grenouillère, Argenteuil, and Vétheuil, and the coasts of Normandy and Brittany, show water activated by waves and currents and described with dashed and overlapping strokes of broken color.[33] However, both moving and still water fascinated Monet throughout his life.[34]

Only in 1896–97 did Monet return to the theme of mirrored waters in the sequence of *Mornings on the Seine*. In the course of a year, he painted from a flatboat approximately twenty canvases of serene, reflecting river vistas.[35] In the present exhibition, the Boston *Morning on the Seine* (cat. 3) exemplifies the series, which commentators have called a tribute to Corot.[36] Their structure, pale palette, and early morning mists recall the older painter, who received a centenary retrospective in Paris in 1895. Monet reportedly remarked in 1897, "There is only one master here—Corot. We are nothing compared to him, nothing."[37] However, in their low, boater's vantage point, watery foregrounds, and simplified formats, the *Mornings* owe as much to Daubigny's riverscapes (fig. 6). Both Daubigny's and Monet's paintings depend for their unified effects on the repeating parallelism of motifs and their reflections. Monet's originality lay in his use of pure colors, broad vaporous strokes, and flattened space, as well as his focus on the momentary, which led to the series paintings.

Finally, in the *Water Lilies*, Monet stepped even closer to the reflecting surface and severed it from its landscape (cats. 6–9). Now very far indeed from Valenciennes's perspective, Monet also retained little of the mid-century landscapists' overlapping spatial planes: just a few tree branches and a drift of lilies appear in their own materiality to suggest the space in front of the pond's glassy surface. The images consist primarily of painted reflections, rich in their complexity, containing dazzling skeins of sky, trees, and light. Now we understand why, late in life, Monet preferred to paint still water. Only a relatively smooth pond would allow him to render, simultaneously, changing surface effects, mirrored surroundings, and depths. His comment, "These landscapes of water and reflections have become an obsession,"[38] alludes to the difficulty of the self-imposed challenge.

The meanings of Monet's water paintings lie perhaps in his evocation of subjective experience, in the exploration of the phenomenology of perception, or in the redefinition of artistic illusion. Indeed, the late pictures stand a long way from his predecessors' water paintings, those windows onto convincing realities, reflecting back human visions of the beautiful, the scenic, and the tranquil. And yet it was Monet's lingering allegiance to those representational and emotional impulses—however expanded and deconstructed—that complicates and fascinates in our readings of the *Water Lilies*. Attempting the impossible, seeking to fix the temporary in a permanent image, Monet carried painting's past into its future.

# FRAGMENTS AND REFLECTIONS

## MONET, WAR, AND ELLEN JOHNSON

*By Andria Derstine*

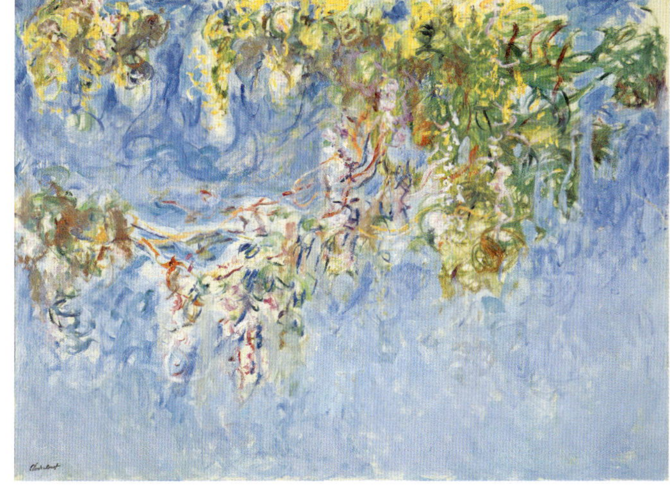

**Cat. 11**
Claude Monet, *Wisteria (Glycines)*, ca. 1919–20, oil on canvas, 59 x 78 7/8 in. (149.8 x 200.5 cm), Allen Memorial Art Museum, Oberlin College, Oberlin, Ohio: R.T. Miller Jr. Fund, 1960 (1960.5)

Monet's *Wisteria* at Oberlin College (cat. 11) is part of a series of canvases depicting that flowering, fragrant, sturdy climber. These paintings were originally meant to hang above the artist's celebrated *Water Lilies*; together they were to constitute his *Grandes Décorations*, the major undertaking of his final years. Beginning to evolve as early as 1897,[1] and by 1909 considered a potential site of repose and meditation,[2] this project eventually became intimately bound up with France's military efforts and the commemoration of her victory in the First World War. The paintings of wisteria were likely painted in or just before 1920. During that summer and fall, planning occurred towards the display of the works in what was to be a circular pavilion on the grounds of the Hôtel Biron. In that same year Monet told the Duc de Trévise that he was working on a wisteria frieze to surmount his water lily series.[3] But the 1921 decision to install them in the Orangerie, due to concerns about the cost of new construction, negated this part of the program, as its walls were not high enough for both water lilies and wisteria.

Monet had settled in Giverny in April 1883, renting a house he was to buy in 1890; in that latter year he began improvements on the property, including—with the purchase of an additional plot of land in 1893—the creation of his water garden.[4] The trellis covered by mauve and white wisteria surmounting his Japanese-style bridge was erected in the earliest years of the new century, and on the far side of the pond grew lavender wisteria.[5] All three colors are evident in the Oberlin painting, celebrated for its lyrical, arabesque strokes, and glowing with light.

The ravages wrought by the First World War—with its dank trenches, grim barbed wire, and extensive combat—quickly included Monet's stepson, Jean-Pierre Hoschedé, and son-in-law, Albert Salerou, being called up, members of Monet's family leaving Giverny for greater safety, and Monet's son Michel entering the army in 1915 and fighting at Verdun the next year. Stretchers bearing the wounded and cannon fire became normal sights and sounds; Monet followed the combat via a map, vowing never to be chased out of his home. Georges Clemenceau, minister of war and then prime minister of France, Monet's best friend, remained a confidant throughout the conflict.[6]

The war's toll proved vastly different from Monet's own earlier experiences with military service. After pulling a low lottery number, he had been drafted, into a light cavalry regiment in Algeria in 1861, an experience he regarded as an adventure: "Nothing attracted me so much as the endless cavalcades under the burning sun, the *razzias*, the crackling of gunpowder, the saber thrusts, the nights in the desert under a tent...I incessantly saw something new...The impressions of light and color that I received there were not to classify themselves until later; but they contained the germ of my future researches."[7] The Franco-Prussian War broke out in July 1870 just weeks after Monet had married his long-time companion, model, and mother of his son, Camille Doncieux. Rather than face the possibility of military service again, as he had been placed on the reserves at his marriage, he left without them for England (they eventually joined him), moving later to Holland to avoid the fighting and upheaval of the Paris Commune that followed the war.[8]

The devastation of the First World War was thus on a vastly greater scale than anything Monet would have yet experienced, and while it is clear that the project of a grand decorated space, meant for repose and meditation amidst paintings inspired by his water garden, was contemplated years before the war—and preparations to carry it out were started in the first half of 1914 before the war's commencement—the project quickly became bound up with the conflict.[9] Important dates in the war effort were even linked to significant moments of its creation: Monet later claimed that he started the paintings on August 1, 1914 (the day that Germany declared war on Russia and on which France refused Germany's demand of neutrality), which, as Paul Tucker has written, "is not true but shows how the war in hindsight informed these paintings;"[10] after the war, authors linked November 18, 1917, the day Allied troops entered Strasbourg, with Clemenceau supposedly accepting Monet's offer of water landscapes as a commemorative gift to the state;[11] and on November 12, 1918, the day following the Armistice, Monet wrote Clemenceau, "I am on the verge of finishing two decorative panels that I want to sign on the day of Victory and am going to ask you to offer them to the State...It's not much, but it is the only way I have of taking part in the victory. I would like these two panels in the Museum of Decorative Arts and would be happy that they were chosen by you."[12] When the Orangerie rooms were at last opened to the public in May 1927, the entrance price of 20 francs—four times the normal amount—was to benefit war widows, another mark of the war's continuing association with the entire effort.[13]

Giverny throughout the war was a haven for Monet, and its lure for others, beginning in Monet's lifetime and continuing thereafter, was great. Ellen Johnson (1910–1992; fig. 9, shown lecturing in front of *Wisteria*), one of Oberlin College's most eminent and inspiring professors, and a universally admired scholar of modern and contemporary art, poignantly recalled her own visit there:

> On...a perfect spring day in Paris, a friend proposed a drive out in the country to visit a friend of his that he was sure I'd like. Imagine my astonished heart when it turned out to be Monsieur Hoschedé, Monet's step son, at Giverny. (That was in 1951, some time before the place became a public trust.) The old gentleman was most amiable, seeming to enjoy greatly taking me through all the buildings, including the house with the room whose walls were still covered with Japanese prints, and the small studio and the large one in which, rolled up against the wall, were one after another of the great huge late paintings. After recounting how the Allies had been stationed on one side of the river Epte and the Germans on the other, firing back and forth at each other, M. Hoschedé pointed out bullet holes in many of the canvasses. He rolled out several of those grand paintings, till finally, struck quite senseless, I asked if there was any chance of Oberlin's purchasing one of them. He said one would have to ask Michel Monet. When I asked how one might reach him, he didn't try to disguise his feelings when he replied, "He's as always out in Africa or somewhere shooting animals!"
>
> The waterlilies were not blossoming yet, but the wisteria branches hung from the bridge as they do so vibrantly in Oberlin's large late painting, and the flower gardens were glorious, even though M. Hoschedé lamented that there was now only one gardener where there had been six in Monet's time. Still I felt, as anyone must when one stands in that place, totally enveloped in Monet's glowing paintings. Strange, the power a garden has to hold and evoke such a presence, somewhat the way a house can retain and reflect not only the behavior toward it of its former inhabitants, but their very character, how they lived their lives. (The power a scent has to carry one straight back into a past experience is not the same; that is just one's own existence, not someone else's.)[14]

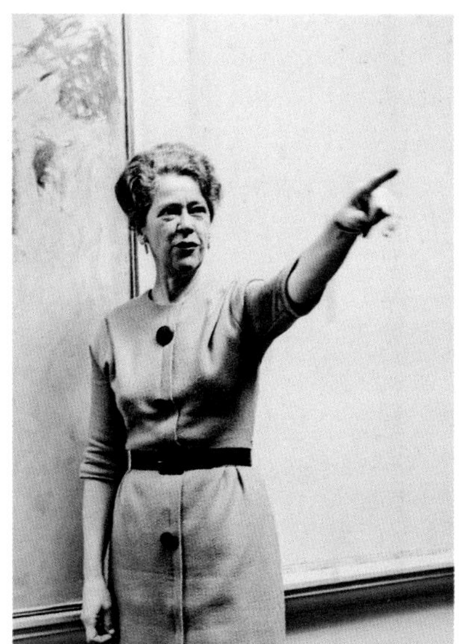

**Fig. 9**
Arthur Princehorn, *Ellen Johnson in front of Monet's Wisteria*, 1964, photograph, courtesy of Oberlin College Archives, with the author's thanks to Franny Brock, Ken Grossi, and Joseph Romano

This powerful remembrance, rich in detail though written some forty years after the visit, does not simply evoke the magic of the place on "a perfect spring day" and the tangible presence of the artist that Johnson felt. It also evidences the contrast between Giverny's role as sanctuary during, and site of commemoration after, the First World War, and the property itself having been physically marked by the weapons of the Second, as was so much of the Norman countryside. William Seitz wrote in 1960 of the works left in Monet's studio being "damaged by shells from tanks and artillery during the Nazi retreat"—as indeed were the very rooms in the Orangerie in which Monet's paintings hung, during the Liberation of Paris in August 1944—and while it is not clear that what Johnson saw were actual bullet holes or more general damage from heavy artillery fire in the area, what is certain is that paintings created alongside those destined to celebrate the Allied victory in 1918 were themselves damaged by the extensive battles of 1944, and, for that time, the idea of Giverny as haven had been shattered.[15] In this passage Johnson too evokes, through the lament of the genial and gracious Jean-Pierre Hoschedé, dismay at time's passage and the degradations this can bring.[16] In the years after Monet's death, not only was Giverny's staff diminished, but so too was its energy.

And yet, the force of the master's presence remained. Johnson's final statement regarding the different, and less intense, power of a scent to carry one back in time is telling, and seems an allusion to Proust's famous passage regarding the smell and taste of tea and madeleines. Proust, for whom remembrance and evocation were all (and for whom, indeed, a madeleine called to mind water lilies floating on a river) was deeply inspired by Monet.[17] Johnson, however, draws a clear line of demarcation between the recollections of one's own past that scent can bring, and one's ability to physically sense the presence of others who have gone before when immersed in their surroundings. As someone who herself lived in and labored for decades on a beautiful, historic property—Oberlin's Frank Lloyd Wright-designed Weltzheimer-Johnson house—she intimately knew the power that such a personal, past physical presence could hold.

Rivers, too, are lines of demarcation, such as the Epte that Hoschedé noted to Johnson was the local boundary over which the Allies and Germans traded bullets, or the dreamy, poetic Vivonne so dear to Proust. The Epte's tributary, the

Ru stream, was the source Monet had diverted, in 1893 and again in 1901, at great cost and with much local bureaucratic wrangling, to create his celebrated pond, the center of his water garden, and a constant source of fresh water for his exotic plants. Monet's lifelong interest in water and all its forms is well known and well documented; streams, rivers, the Channel, the Mediterranean, rain, snow, ice, fog, mist, clouds—even the steam of trains and above all his water garden—were among his primary inspirations. For Johnson, as well, a river provided a turning point as regards a life spent with art, as she recalled, thinking back to circa 1915, near the Allegheny River on the outskirts of Warren, in northwestern Pennsylvania:

> I was about five years old...I was standing on the porch in the late afternoon... looking out across the river and the island. I'd just had a bath and had on a fresh dress and my hair was all brushed and combed. I felt so clean and so much a part of the beautiful sky and trees, and I was looking over the hills across the river. I think that's when I first became interested in art.[18]

She described the same experience in slightly different terms in her memoirs:

> One of my very first clear memories is decidedly a body-sensory one, and I've also long considered it as my first aesthetic experience....I felt the river in the air all around me...It must have just rained, because everything looked so sparkling fresh: the grass, Mamma's flowers, and the bushes and trees and the island and the hill that rose steeply behind it. It was early evening and everything was still....As I stood there looking out over the river to the hill rising straight up above it, I felt as clean and as good as everything around me. For the first time I was conscious of my body in relation to and a part of a complete and rounded and quite wonderful whole. Of course I didn't know the word for it, but it was harmony I felt.[19]

This harmony, brought about by the relation of rain and river water with grass, flowers, bushes, and trees, and her own presence amidst them, together with the sky and the freshness of the surrounding landscape, was a defining moment. For it linked visual perception and bodily immersion in nature to art and aesthetics, as was certainly the case for Monet throughout his lifetime, and especially, in his final decades, as he worked in his water garden. Such a forceful feeling, like the urgency of Monet's own impressions, was engendered by immediacy—by a fleeting moment of time—captured here in words, as Monet did in colors.

Time's fluidity can be seen too in the back-and-forth quality of Johnson's *Fragments*, which as a volume weaves together recollections from many decades without progressing linearly (as for Proust's own meditations in his many-layered *Remembrance*). This is evoked in the first passage cited above, in which she recalls asking whether Oberlin might purchase one of the large works, and is told she must track down Michel Monet, but then swiftly mentions Oberlin's "large late painting." Indeed Oberlin did acquire *Wisteria*, a painting she had quite possibly seen that day, as it remained in Monet's studio and was the property of Monet's son after the artist's death. The acquisition, however, did not occur until 1960, nine years after her visit. In the intervening time, the late works that remained in the studio had been "discovered," with a number being shown at Katia Granoff's gallery in Paris in 1956 and 1957. Johnson's remembrance thus gains added importance in that her visit came some five years before Monet's late works were publicly known. These paintings were a revelation, coming into view following the Second World War and what had been a progressive waning of interest in Impressionism from the 1910s through the 1940s, when a veritable succession of other "isms" took hold. Their radical qualities and profusion of tangled brushstrokes quickly became bound up with the nascent discourse on Abstract Expressionism, and they came to be seen as pioneering forays by the great artist at the end of his life.[20]

**Fig. 10**
Claude Monet, *Garden of the Princess, Louvre (Le Jardin de l'Infante)*, 1867, oil on canvas, 36 1/8 x 24 3/8 in. (91.8 x 61.9 cm), Allen Memorial Art Museum, Oberlin College, Oberlin, Ohio, R.T. Miller Jr. Fund, 1948 (1948.296)

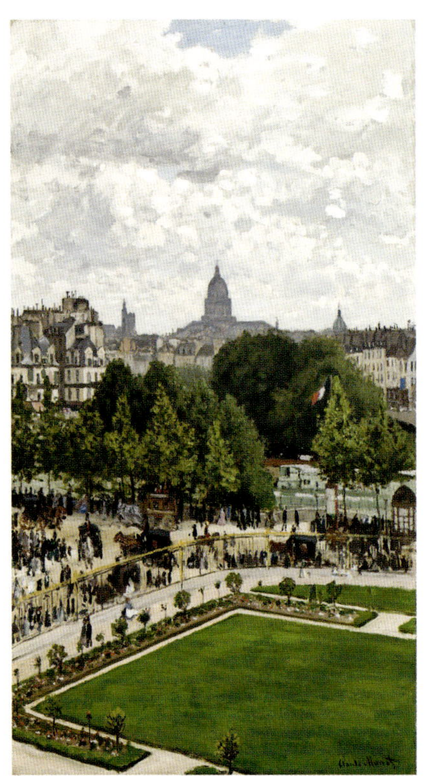

Monet's monumental paintings of wisteria, blossoms that were but a part of the dense foliage of bamboo, weeping willows, and other trees and plants in his garden, certainly are not literal views. Their poetry and energy come not only from the broadness and quickness of their strokes, but also from the placement of the flowers and vines against a brilliant blue sky created with variegated colors and, almost like water, itself apparently roiling and in flux. The paintings seem almost to imply a view straight up, of wisteria and wisteria alone against the sky—neither trellis nor arbor can be seen, and there is no interference from trees or other background foliage. Far removed in spirit from one of Monet's most serene garden views, Oberlin's *Garden of the Princess, Louvre* (fig. 10)

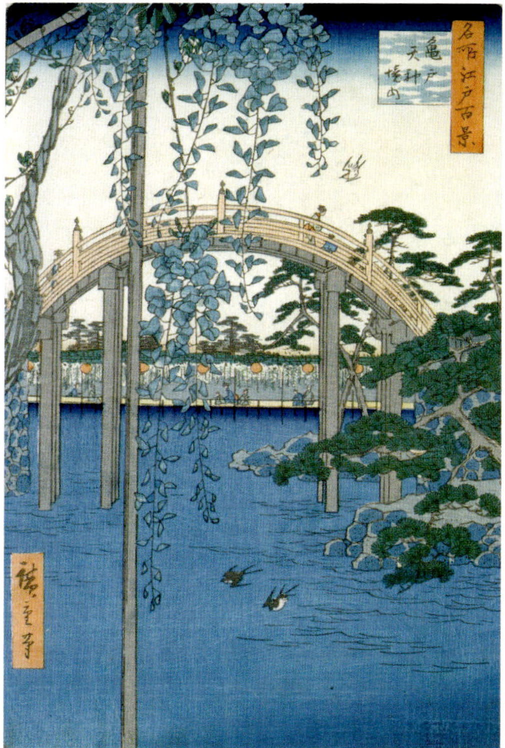


**Fig. 11**
Utagawa Hiroshige, *The Drum Bridge from the Wisteria Arbor on the Precincts of the Tenjin Shrine at Kameido*, no. 57 from the series *One Hundred Views of Famous Places in Edo*, 1856, color woodblock print, 13 3/4 x 9 1/16 in. (34.9 x 23 cm), Allen Memorial Art Museum, Oberlin College, Oberlin, Ohio, Mary A. Ainsworth Bequest (1950.1421)

—with its expansive sky over a recognizable urban scene created over fifty years earlier—their facture too is far removed from what may have been one element in their inspiration, a print by Utagawa Hiroshige (fig. 11) showing an arched wooden bridge behind cascading vines of lavender wisteria.[21] Their rhythmic brushwork and medley of looping, quasi-ethereal garlands carry forward to the early twentieth century, as to the early twenty-first. It is a vision seemingly reminiscent of other places and times, of exotic plants presumably attached to the land and drawing life from water, but unanchored and reaching, like Victory proffering a crown, towards the bright, midday heavens. Taking part both in the beauty of nature and in the relief that followed the First World War, their radical, expansive qualities, like those of Monet's other late paintings, were only finally recognized by Johnson and others, following the Second World War.

# FROM INSTANT TO *ENVELOPPE*

## REFLECTIONS ON MONET, PHOTOGRAPHY, AND TIME

*By Beth E. Wilson*

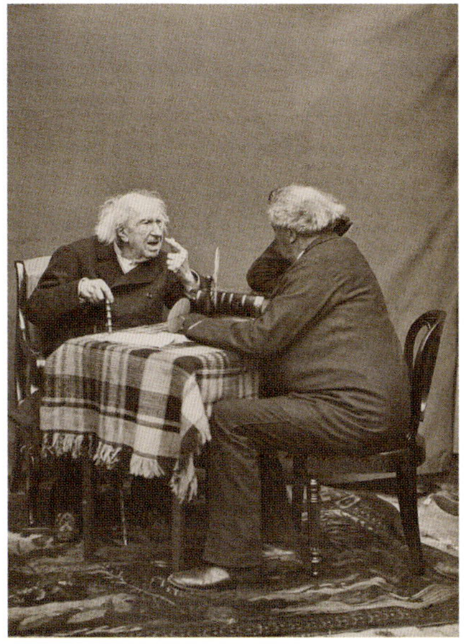
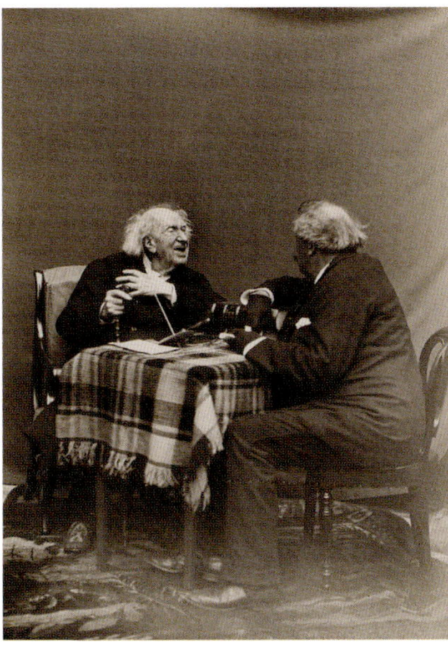

**Fig. 12**
Paul Nadar, *M. Félix Nadar Interviews M. Michel Eugène Chevreul on his Hundredth Birthday*, 1886, albumen prints, Courtesy of George Eastman House, International Museum of Photography and Film (1977:0033:26 and 1977:0033:33)

On August 31, 1886, the renowned photographer Félix Nadar visited the chemist Michel Eugène Chevreul on the occasion of his hundredth birthday. Accompanying Nadar was his son, Paul, who photographed their conversation, in a series of twenty-seven negatives, capturing the lively expressions and gesticulations of the centenarian scientist. A selection of twenty-one of these images was published in September 1886 in the popular *Journal illustré*, accompanied by captions provided by Nadar, summarizing M. Chevreul's remarks (fig. 12). In the history of photography, this is often cited as the first photographic interview ever published.

I have used these images of Chevreul and Nadar as a starting point to discuss Claude Monet's work for several reasons. First, Chevreul's major contribution to science had been his publication of his law of simultaneous contrast (in 1839, the same year that Daguerre first unveiled his successful photographic process in Paris), in which he recognized the perceptual influence that various colors have upon each other, a theory that reverberated through much artistic practice well into the twentieth century. Despite Monet's frequent disavowal of any intellectual or scientific theory of painting, the one such concept he ever seems to have mentioned aloud is this one. Indeed, it would probably have been difficult to discuss with other artists the sorts of aesthetic experiments with color that he pursued in the 1880s and beyond without some recourse to Chevreul, so deeply embedded had this scientific argot become in the vocabulary of his contemporaries.[1]

The other person appearing in the interview photographs, Nadar, also figures prominently in the history of Impressionism. Born Gaspard Félix Tournachon, he began as a caricaturist for the popular press in the 1840s, changing his *métier* to photography in the 1850s. His enormously successful portrait practice grew to occupy an entire building at 35, Boulevard des Capucines in Paris, on one floor of which he allowed a group of artist friends to show their work in 1874—the first of what thereafter were called the "Impressionist Exhibitions." (It was at this first group show that, much to the painter's chagrin, the title of Monet's *Impression: Sunrise* was seized upon by a hostile critic who then dubbed the group "Impressionists.")

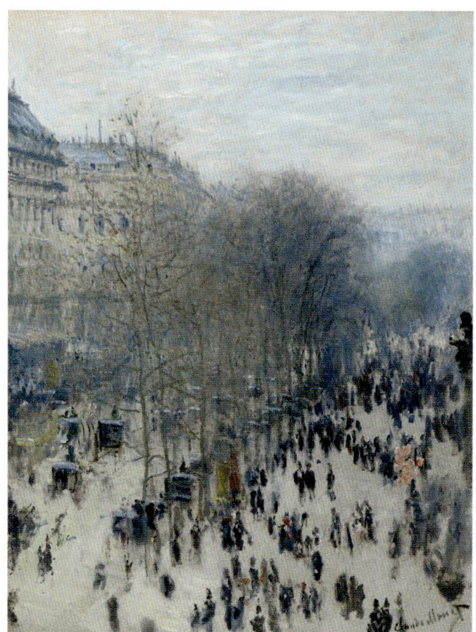

**Fig. 13**
Claude Monet, *Boulevard des Capucines*, 1873–74, oil on canvas, 31 5/8 x 23 3/4 in. (80.3 x 60.3 cm), The Nelson-Atkins Museum of Art, Kansas City, Missouri. Purchase: The Kenneth A. and Helen F. Spencer Foundation Acquisition Fund (F72-35)

There is more to the relationship between Monet and photography than the mere accident of the location of his movement's appellation; however, just as with his refusal to admit (at least publicly) his dependence on even rudimentary elements of color theory, the artist remained noticeably silent on the insights he might have drawn from the new medium. It is my contention here that even though there is little direct evidence in his public statements or correspondence on the subject, it is possible to infer a relationship between Monet's painting and photography, especially as the latter grew to be such a fundamental component of visual culture in the second half of the nineteenth century.

Aaron Scharf was the first scholar to note the similarity between the blurred figures in motion appearing in popular photographic views taken in Paris in the 1860s and 1870s and the blurring of figures seen in the foreground of Monet's painting of the *Boulevard des Capucines*, made in 1873–74 (fig. 13).[2] At this early point in his career, it certainly appears that Monet felt free to apply an effect found in photography to communicate the bustling foot traffic on the *grand boulevard*—in a painting that was made, by the way, from the vantage point of Nadar's studio.

Much later, however, Monet seems to express a very different, almost hostile relationship to photography, at least as far as it was implicated in his own work. In a

1905 letter to his dealer Durand-Ruel, the artist responded angrily to the accusation by two English artists that he, in fact, had relied on photographs for some of his recent London paintings, asserting that

> ...whether my Cathedrals, my Londons and other canvasses were painted from life or not is nobody's business and totally unimportant. I know so many painters who paint only from life and who produce nothing but horrors....[3]

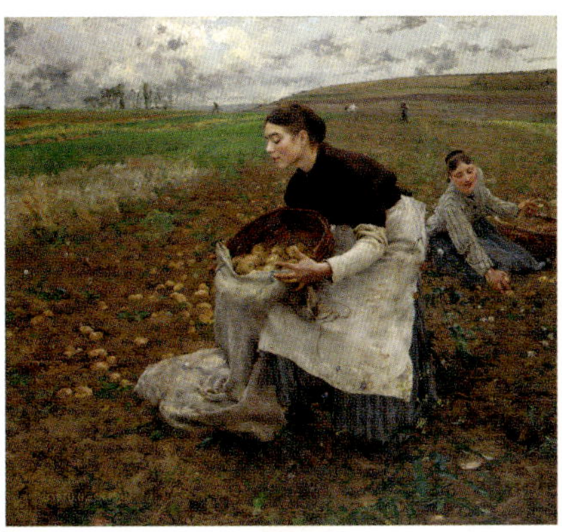

**Fig. 14**
Jules Bastien-Lepage, *October*, 1878, oil on canvas, 71 7/8 x 77 3/16 in. (180.7 x 196 cm), National Gallery of Victoria, Melbourne, Felton Bequest, 1928 (3678-3)

It is interesting to note that Monet here is not so much asserting the *plein air* purity of his pictures (which by this point he was starting *ad vivum*, but then extensively working over later in the studio), as he is distancing himself from what might be understood as a photographically conditioned mode of representation, understood as presenting the world in a meticulous and overwhelming profusion of detail. It is precisely this aesthetic that underpins the academic practice of what is often referred to as Naturalism in the last third of the nineteenth century, seen here in *October*, a Salon painting made by Jules Bastien-Lepage in 1878 (fig. 14). The sharp focus and extremely detailed rendering found in this work reflects Bastien-Lepage's openly acknowledged emulation of visual effects drawn from photography.

For Monet, this sort of Naturalism is the path not taken. It is worth noting that in the *Boulevard des Capucines* picture, the element of photography that Monet chooses to emulate is, in fact, the result of the medium's very inability to freeze and focus the detail of the figures in motion below. Thinking through this choice leads us to the key concept linking photography and Monet's practice: *instantaneity*. We must be careful before we leap to a conclusion about what exactly that term means, however. The notion of the "instant" is one that developed historically, a reflection of various technological advances and cultural conceptions over time. Today, most people probably think of an instant as a fraction of a second, something that takes place in the time it takes to snap one's fingers. But even within photography, such a temporally constricted instant was not technically possible, at least not until the 1880s, when the gelatin silver (or "dry plate") process came into widespread use. The new gelatin silver emulsions, in addition to providing much greater flexibility in exposure and development of the negative, also had the advantage of a much higher sensitivity to light; thus, it was possible for the first time to capture (and to freeze) motion at speeds much faster than the human eye could follow. In fact, it was not until the advent of dry plate that cameras required mechanical shutters—up to this time, photographers exposed their plates by simply removing the lens cap, waiting for the appropriate length of time, and then replacing it.

It is worth mentioning here that *plein air* landscape practice, emphasizing the immediacy of the painter's experience, first came to prominence during precisely the same few decades at the beginning of the nineteenth century in which two dozen or more individuals—often with no knowledge of each other—felt compelled to devise photochemical means to capture and record the ephemeral images of the camera obscura. In both cases, the desire to fix these fleeting images depends upon a newly emerging cultural conception of time, and the related epistemological drive to arrest and hold onto a particular moment from it—in other words, at the outset, there was a deep link between photography and *plein air* landscape practice, at the level of what we might identify as *instantaneity*, understood (at least initially) as it was experienced within the bounds of normal human perception.

During the first part of Monet's career, this earlier, more attenuated photographic instant would have been the common experience of the medium.

Monet's early work in the 1860s and 1870s emphasized relatively quick execution directly from the motif, reproducing in paint an analogue of his visual "impressions" of the scene before him. In *The Seine at Port-Villez*, 1883–90 (cat. 1), we see this *plein air* method in full force. Relatively quickly executed, most likely on the spot from the middle of the river in his studio boat, his translation of the trees caressed by the wind and the flow of the river in the foreground focuses on the play and relationship of color, certainly, but the lack of tight focus registers not only the relative speed of the painting's execution, but also a somewhat elastic relationship to the flow of time, as seen in the blurred movement of the elements of his motif.

In the 1880s, after his move to Giverny, Monet's practice becomes much more complex.[4] In response to what seems to have been a growing frustration with trying to paint within the gap between the moment of perception and its representation on the canvas, he adopted a more recursive practice, "laying in" the landscape directly from the motif, then correcting (later, "harmonizing") the colors, overall balance of the picture, etc. in the studio, before declaring the work finished to his satisfaction.

This hybrid practice becomes institutionalized in Monet's series paintings of the early 1890s, represented here by the *Poplars*, 1891 (cat. 2). In 1877, Monet had anticipated the later, full-blown series work in a group of paintings of the Gare Saint-

Lazare railway station, which frame the atmospheric clouds of steam from the engines within the strikingly modern architectonics of the glass-roofed train shed. Yet despite this rather ambitious first attempt at an iconic, monumental series of related paintings, Monet did not return to the idea of working in series until he started painting the *Grainstacks* in the fields near his home in Giverny in 1890. What had happened in the interim, and how might we explain his return, after thirteen years, to the idea of series paintings—and not only a group of paintings of the same motif, but series that in the 1890s are much more systematic in approach, and often discussed as representing specific times of day, seasons, and/or particular lighting conditions?

One significant development taking place squarely in the gap between the Gare Saint-Lazare paintings and the later, more systematized series works of the 1890s was the advent of chronophotography (the photographic analysis of motion). In the early 1880s, French scientist Étienne-Jules Marey was inspired by the example of Eadweard Muybridge's photographic studies of galloping horses to analyze movement across a series of photographic exposures. These chronophotographic studies became widely known in the 1880s, through both scientific and popular journals, and through the publication of illustrated books such as Muybridge's *Animal Locomotion* in 1886. The major advances in this new field, while begun using the old collodion/wet plate process in the late 1870s, were dramatically facilitated with the introduction of the much faster gelatin silver process. George Eastman's innovation of applying the gelatin silver emulsion to a flexible roll of paper was used by Marey to quickly shoot a series of negatives that froze various stages of movement that were otherwise invisible to the naked eye. He also began photographing multiple exposures on a single plate, as seen here in his study of a pelican in flight (fig. 15).

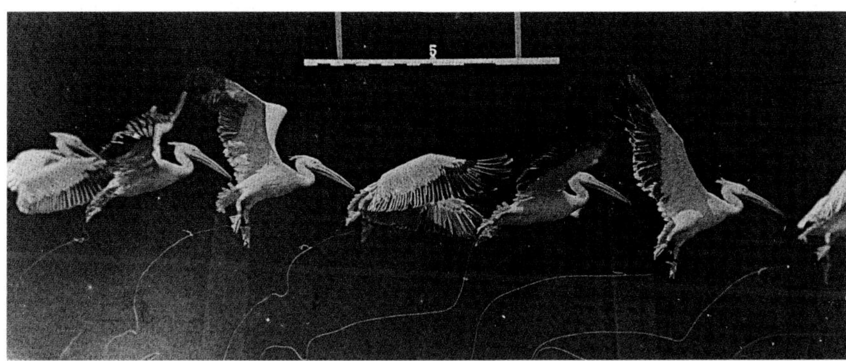


**Fig. 15**
Étienne-Jules Marey, *Pelican in Flight*, ca. 1882, chronophotography, albumen silver print, Collection of the Cinémathèque française (42125)

Seriality became something of a visual virus throughout the 1880s, applied photographically not only in scientific work such as Marey's analysis of motion or Charcot's medical work charting the postures of hysterics, but also in popular contexts such as the Nadar/Chevreul interview cited above, as well as in the striking series of photographs by Théophile Féau documenting the erection of the Eiffel Tower in the months leading up to the 1889 Exposition Universelle in Paris, to name but a few examples.

These serial images break down and transform the older conception of the lived instant, reorganizing temporal experience in ways that transcend the normal capacities of the human eye: placing them in sequence, it became possible to synthesize a new visual experience, whether expanding the perception of time in the motion studies, or collapsing it in Féau's "time-lapse" images. The next logical step, of course, was the development of the motion picture, a medium that reconstructs (synthesizes) the movement otherwise so artificially arrested in the still chronophotographic image.[5]

Monet anticipated exactly this shift in his hybrid painting practice, by first registering the immediacy of his motif *en plein air* (analysis), then summarizing the results by reworking the canvases in his studio, generating a synthesis reproducing his experience, more broadly understood. He worked his way to this new temporal conception by expanding the *plein air* instant to encompass the concept of the *enveloppe*, which is typically discussed as the envelope of light and atmosphere surrounding his motifs. As he wrote to Gustave Geffroy in 1890,

> The further I go, the better I see that it takes a great deal of work to succeed in rendering what I want to render: "instantaneity", above all the *enveloppe*, the same light spread over everything, and I'm more than ever disgusted at things that come easily, at the first attempt.[6]



I would contend that this *enveloppe* extends beyond simply the play of light and atmosphere, and must be understood temporally (as Monet himself here seems to say), in terms of duration as well. The impossible gap presented by *plein air* practice is that between the ever-shifting light and the fixed nature of the marks placed on the canvas: how is one ever to keep up, even in as short a passage of time as a half-hour? With the development of his *enveloppe*, Monet dilates the *plein air* instant into a phenomenologically rich duration of time, one in which the human eye can take its time to notice the colors, the flickers of light, as they arise and pass from consciousness. In essence, he shifts from analyzing, breaking down the immediacy of the visual in the earlier *plein air* work, toward a richer synthesis of perceptual experience, more holistically understood. (In this context, it is interesting to note that when visiting Giverny in person, the water garden in particular is alive with buzzing insect life, none of which ever finds its way into Monet's paintings; it was Marey the scientist, after all, who was interested in freezing the motion of animal life.) It must be understood that Monet's perceptual moment is not a naïve one: this duration is absolutely dependent on the existence of a well-steeped knowledge of the world and the representational logic(s) of the pictorial, including of course things like the artist's oft-mentioned extensive collection of Japanese prints, but which in the late nineteenth century most certainly also included the ubiquitous experience of photography as one of its significant constituents.

And so Monet's later work, developing after his move to Giverny, is far from a direct transcription of the mere appearance of that place. One could argue that the post-1900 paintings of the water garden, the *Nymphéas* (cats. 6–9), are really not so much paintings of the pond itself as they are recursive, mediated views of the reflected sky, clouds, and overhanging willows. Eliminating the horizon line, Monet focuses his attention on the landscape as seen upside-down on the surface of the water, a framing ironically reminiscent of the inverted image found on a photographer's ground glass; filtering this view through a lifetime of rich, nuanced, and informed aesthetic ruminations on time and place, these pictures then offer a much deeper opportunity for reflection than they are often given.

# MONET AND GIVERNY

## *L'ART DANS LES DEUX MONDES* (MARCH 7, 1891)

*Octave Mirbeau*
*Translated by Benedict Leca*

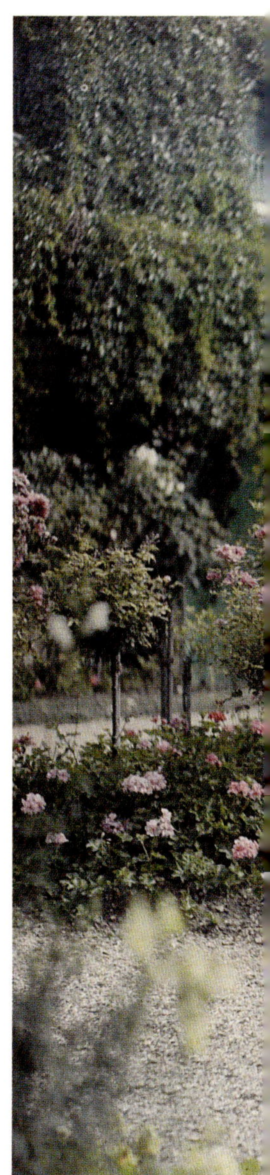

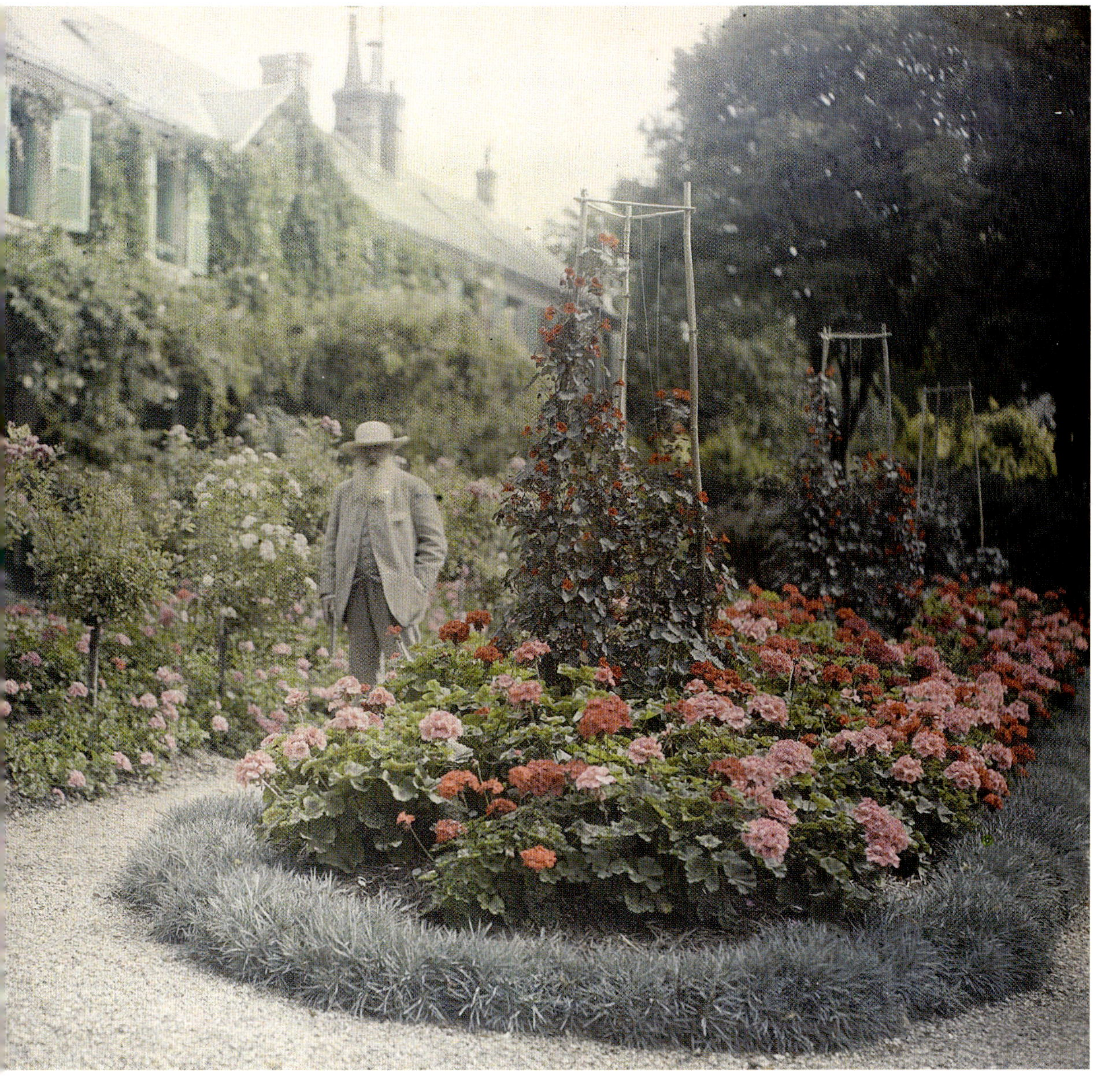

Fig. 16 (previous page)
Anonymous, *Claude Monet in Front of his House at Giverny*, 1921, autochrome, 7 1/16 x 9 7/16 in. (18 x 24 cm), Musée d'Orsay, Paris, France (PHO 2006 9 1)

Fig. 17
Anonymous, *Claude Monet in his Garden at Giverny*, ca. 1925, photograph, Musée Marmottan, Paris, France / Giraudon / Bridgeman Art Library International (MMT161081)

A house roughcast in pink mortar, at the back of a garden always shimmering with flowers.

IT IS SPRING.

The wallflowers are exhaling their last aromas; the peonies—the divine peonies—are faded; the hyacinths are dead. Already the nasturtiums and the poppies (eschscholtzias) divulge themselves: the ones their young shoots of bronze, the others their linear leaves of a delicious, acidic green; and in the big flower beds that they line, in the far reaches of a flowery orchard, irises raise their curved petals strangely trimmed with white, mauve, lilac, yellow, and blue, striated with various dark colors and crimson accents, evoking, in their intricate undersides, mysterious analogies, alluring and perverse dreams, the same as those that float around the disquieting orchids... At the top of their supple stalks, daylilies (hemerocallis) incline their fragrant calyxes; and the poppies reveal enormous sections of blood vermillion on their velutinous peduncles, as they wrap themselves around the horizontal stakes; the clematises highlight the ambient greenery with their large

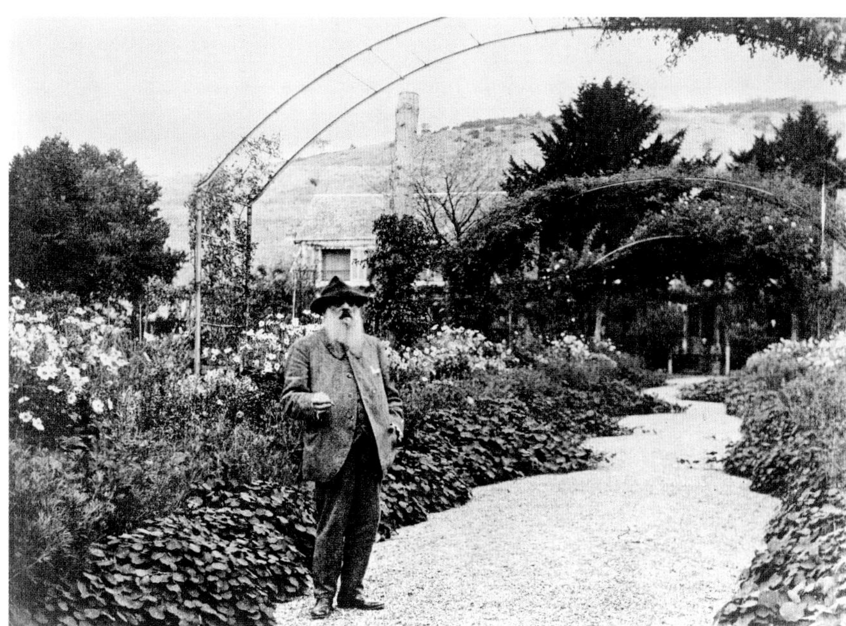

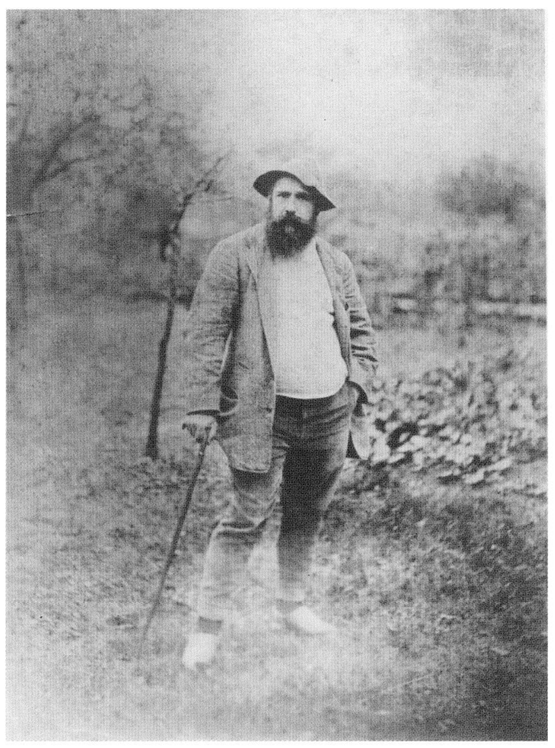

**Fig. 18**
Theodore Robinson, *Claude Monet*, ca. 1889–90, photograph, Archives Durand-Ruel (Photo 16219)

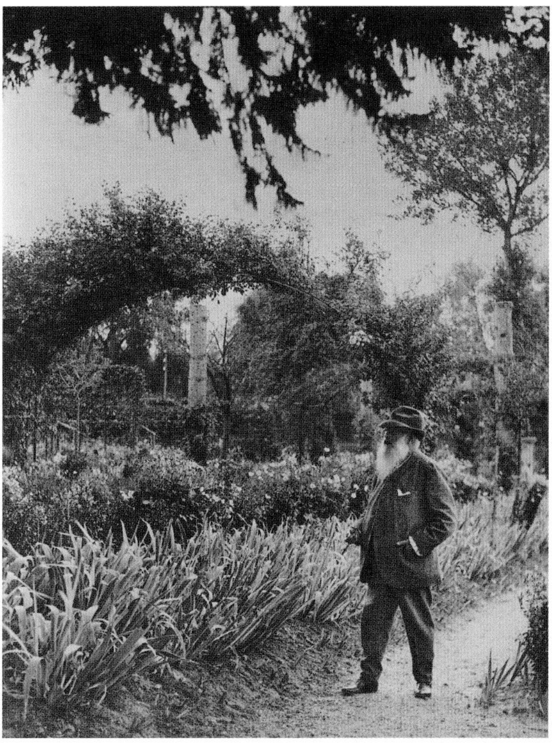

**Fig. 19**
Anonymous, *Claude Monet at Giverny*, ca. 1923–24, photograph, Archives Durand-Ruel (Photo 17286)

flowers, the sky with their immaculate pale corolla, washed with blue azure and touches of pink. And the summer plants, which stir in between the borders, prepare themselves for the joy of flowering.

IT IS SUMMER.

The multicolored nasturtiums and the saffron-colored poppies (eschscholtzias) collapse on either side of the sandy path in a blinding tumble. The striking extravaganza of poppies swells and covers over the deflowered irises in the large flower beds—an extraordinary mixture of tints, an orgy of bright nuances, a resplendent and musical excess of white, pink, yellow, mauve; an incredible kneaded mass of blond flesh upon which orange tones explode, where ardent copper colors resound in flourishes, where reds bleed and ignite, purples jubilate, and blackened scarlets smolder. And here and there, emerging from the marvelous rippling, from this wondrous floral outpouring, the hollyhocks bedeck their stems with exquisite ruffled fabrics of the same vaporous lightness as gauze, of the same brilliant creases as satin, and affix thereupon little dancer's skirts, which puff out and expand. And the Texas sunflowers extend their long leaflets laden with buds, while the large sunflowers (helianthus) from California lunge forward, thrusting their green eye forth from their golden, tousled cowls reminiscent of fabulous irascible birds. And in the air passes the fresh breath of residues that mix with the peppery odors of the nasturtiums.

IT IS FALL.

The nasturtiums have overrun the pathway, and their flowers, which have multiplied boundlessly and are even more dazzling, have overrun the greenery that has yellowed. Supplanting the enchantment of the poppies is the enchantment of the luxurious dahlias, their fluted collarets preciously edged with fine gold, of a liquid purple and soft lilac; bearing pompoms imbricated with all bright colors and their discreet nuances; like stars that shimmer and scintillate atop frail stems, branching out with a charm of light and brazen grace; or else as jagged silhouettes of old silk, of light tones and deliciously faded lace accents; or else as monstrous plumes whose segmented petals taper, spread out, twist into scarlet tassels. At their bases, the asters produce the radiant freshness of their antique ruffs of lace; the antirrhinums put a shine on the striped bicolored velvet of their beastly mask; the Japanese anemones, with a liturgical attitude, dangle their svelte, white corollas and cornets; the phloxes smile like candid corymbs through the multitude of their innocent little eyes; the

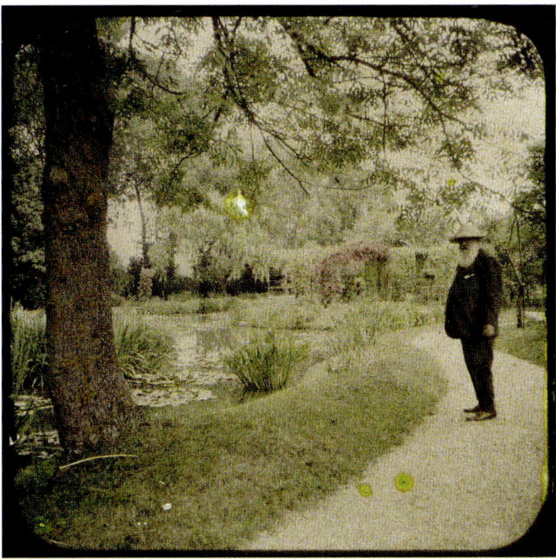

**Fig. 20**
Étienne Clémentel, *Claude Monet in Profile Standing in Front of the Water Lilies, Garden of Giverny*, ca. 1920, autochrome, 1 3/4 x 4 1/8 in. (4.5 x 10.5 cm), Musée d'Orsay, Paris, France (PHO 1988 2 2)

late-coming gladiolas prop up their sumptuous calyxes, tender their lily throats to the enamored buzzing of bees. And in the air filled with all of these reflections, of all these rustlings, of all these pollens, the vertiginous sunflowers turn their yellow disks, ablaze and glittering, and the upraised tufts of the sunflowers (harpaliums) shed the never-ending gold of their inexhaustible blossoming.

And behind the house roughcast in pink mortar arise hills of undulating contours, of slopes draped with the shifting, mottled effects of the harvests; and in front of the garden, still dazzling with flowers, lie vast, deep, successive prairies, prairies where the rows of poplars recede as in an alluring dream in the misty haze of the Norman atmosphere; prairies where the Epte unwinds sinuously, mellifluously, between shady banks, golden colonnades bearing flexible arcs and airy vaults, from which hangs the balanced grace of vines and the shifty whim of hops.

It is here, in this perpetual feast for the eyes, that Claude Monet lives. And it is surely the environment that one imagines for this prodigious painter of the splendid life of color, for this prodigious poet of tender lights and veiled forms, for he who would make exhilarating and perfumed paintings that breathe, who knew how to grasp the intangible, express the inexpressible, and who imbued our dream with the entire mysterious dream enclosed in nature, of the entire dream mysteriously scattered in divine light.

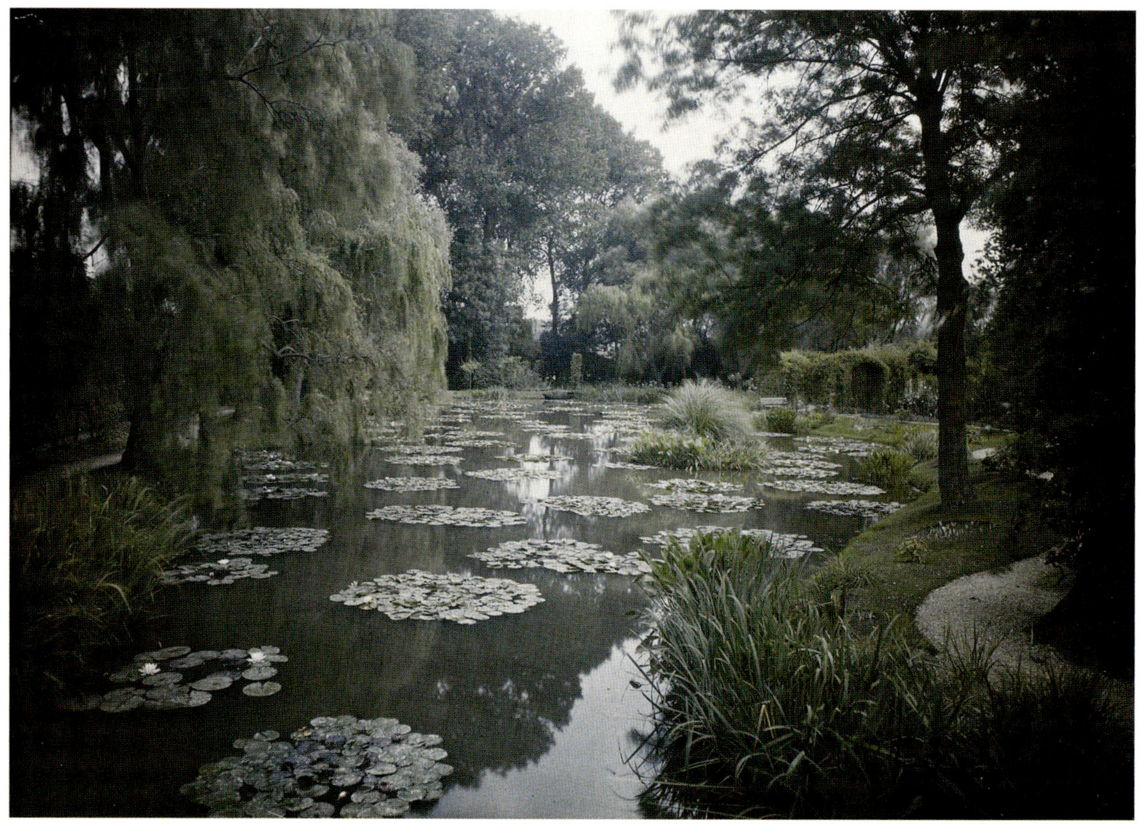

**Fig. 21**
Anonymous, *Water Lily Pond at Giverny*, 1921, autochrome, 7 1/6 x 9 7/16 in. (18 x 24 cm), Musée d'Orsay, Paris, France (PHO 2006 9 2)

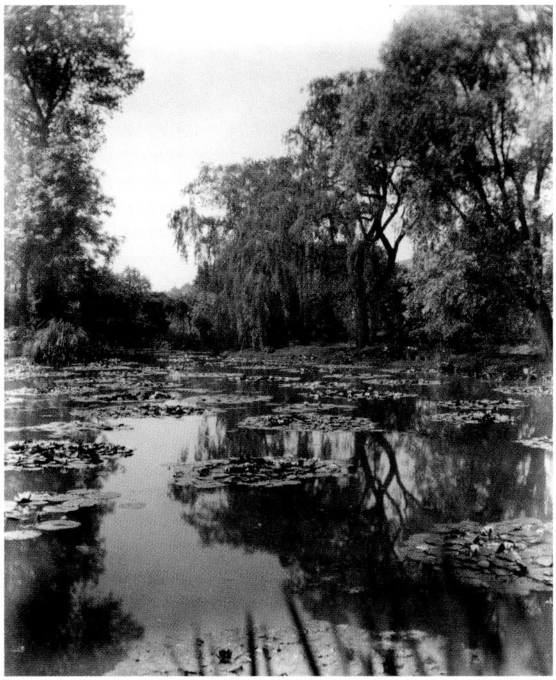

**Fig. 22**
Nickolas Muray, *Monet's Garden at Giverny, France*, 1926, gelatin silver print, 9 5/8 x 7 11/16 in. (24.4 x 19.5 cm), Courtesy of George Eastman House, International Museum of Photography and Film, Gift of Nickolas Muray Family (77:0188:2048)

I have said that this is the environment that we like to imagine for Claude Monet. But has he not, in a way, made all of the environments that he has traversed his own through his immediate intelligence in discovering their peculiar genius, in expressing magnificently their special poetry, in penetrating their exact and deep significance? Did he not make them his by harmonizing his mind, his sensibility to their particular nature, by means of an admirable and almost unique faculty (one that is ordinarily the product of longstanding habits and of patient observations) that he has to extract in a glance the essence of form and of color, and I would say also of the intellectual life, of thought, at this fleeting hour, at this supreme minute of concentrated harmony when dream becomes reality? Do we not imagine him at home, at the edge of the gray and misty seas of the English Channel, on the tragic rocks and howling chasms of Belle-Île (fig. 23), as well as on the calm banks of the Seine or beneath the quivering shades of the Epte? And in the somber gorges of the Creuse, beneath the shorn hillsides of abrupt slopes and granite bulges, or near the churning torrent, where odd, sinister, solitary houses flaunt their murderous gaze, can we not imagine him at home there no less than in flowering orchards and peaceable prairies, where fresh breezes rustle the poplars; where all of the gaieties and joys of the earth and sky unfold through dim hazes? And who better than the painter of western fogs, of snowy winters encrusted with frost, of the great and terrible rhythms of the ocean; who indeed better than this minstrel inspired by rosy springs, pearly dawns, and transparent waters of shifting highlights, has been able to understand and render the hardened soils and the immense deserts of the southern skies; the glossy foliages, the bronze contortions of olive trees, and all of this classical décor, theatrical, grand and dry, where we seemingly still hear the voices of Virgil and Lucian?

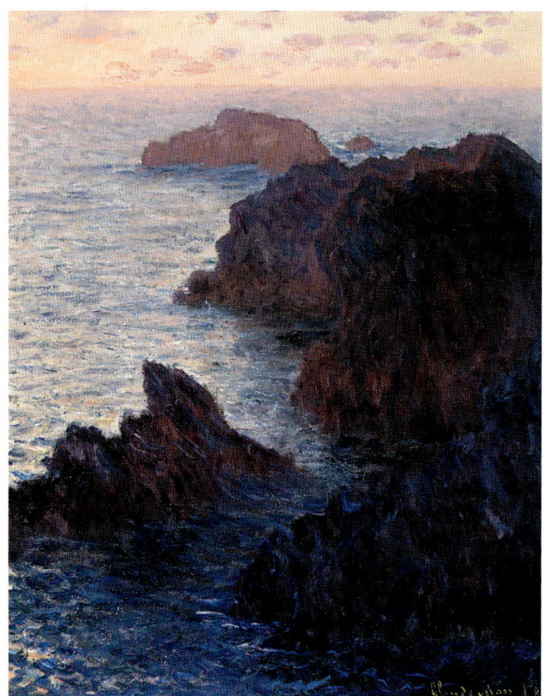

**Fig. 23**
Claude Monet, *Rocks at Belle-Île, Port-Domois*, 1886, oil on canvas, 32 x 25 1/2 in. (81.3 x 64.8 cm), Cincinnati Art Museum, Fanny Bryce Lehmer Endowment and The Edwin and Virginia Irwin Memorial (1985.282)

What can one say about Claude Monet that hasn't been said and repeated a thousand times in France as well as in England, in Belgium, America, and Germany? The public today must surely know the ideal of this art and the impact of its meaning and regenerative influence upon contemporary painting. And if the public does not know it will never know it. Thus why even attempt to have it learn? The public experiences the impulse of a fashion rather than the consequence of a reasoned impression, and what it desires of painters is that they be famous. Yet Claude Monet is now famous, of a hard-won fame gained with pain and difficulty. Criticism, even the most tardigrade, and painter, even the most jealous, no longer dare to contest the enormous power and infinite charm of his works. His exhibitions have this that is particular and utterly spiritual to them: they serve as painting lessons, so to speak, for painters who initially showed themselves to be the most blind, the most hostile to this innovative and thrilling art, which had surpassed the restricted sphere of their intellect. One can see painters, some among the most recognized, painters decorated the length of their lapel, painters that have been rewarded as much as show animals, stop at length in front of each canvas, to apprehend the details, to try to penetrate into the procedures, believing that it might be possible to acquire, through a few superficial revelations of craft, this chosen soul that shudders before all of the beauties of pantheistic life, and this miraculous eye which tames the sun, that goes forth into the unexplored and the invisible, conquering unknown forms and the new language of light. And I think that before works such as these, which call to mind the most noble, elevated, and distant ideas purely by means of the eyes, the critic must renounce his thin, dry, and sterile analyses, with only the poet having the right to speak and to sing. For Claude Monet, who does not bring any direct literary preoccupations to his compositions, is among all painters, alongside perhaps Puvis de Chavannes, the one who addresses himself the most directly, the most eloquently to poets. It is a delicious and poignant promenade full of intellectual surprises, to follow him in this nature recreated by his incomparable genius; in this passionate, moving, fluid nature, where, among the tender sensualities, lies the dream, there at every step, which seizes and draws one towards the mysterious, profound, and always novel celebration of the hours. What is enchanting in Claude Monet's work is that while evidently a realist, he does not limit himself to translating nature and her chromatic and plastic harmonies. Just as in a human face, we see and feel in his works the successive emotions, the latent passions, the moral jolts, the eruptions of interior joy, the melancholies, the pains—everything that nature stirs within us through animistic force, everything beyond us in nature that is marked as infinite and eternal. The landscapes of Claude Monet are, so to speak, the illumination of states of consciousness of the planet as well as the extrasensory forms of our thoughts. To diversify our impressions would he not need to vary his motifs and to change his décors? In fact, the same motif—as in the astounding

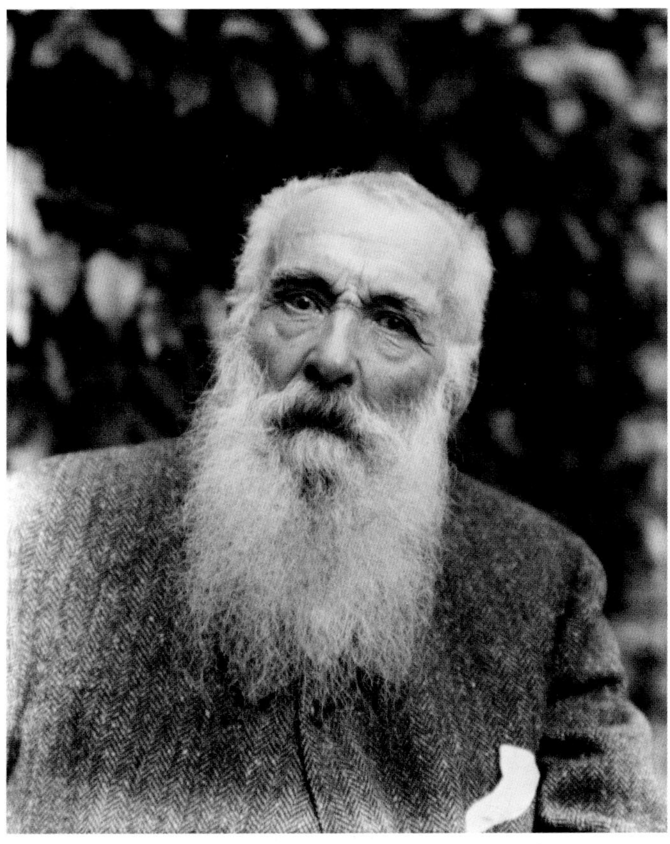

**Fig. 24**
Nickolas Muray, *Claude Monet*, 1926, gelatin silver print, 10 x 8 in. (25.4 x 20.3 cm), Courtesy George Eastman House, International Museum of Photography and Film, Gift of Mrs. Nickolas Muray (77:0188:2034C)

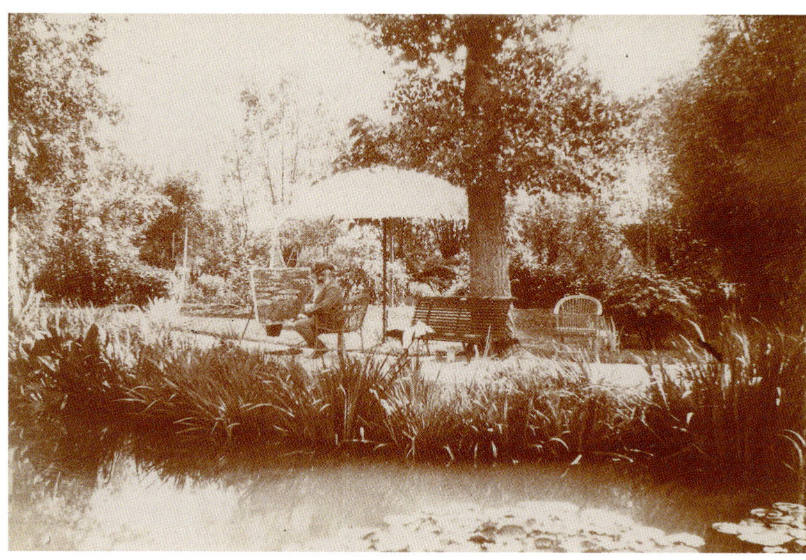

**Fig. 25**
Anonymous, *Claude Monet Working at the Edge of the Water Lily Pond, Giverny*, Summer 1904, sepia gelatin silver print, 2 3/16 x 3 1/16 in. (5.6 x 7.7 cm), Philippe Piguet Collection

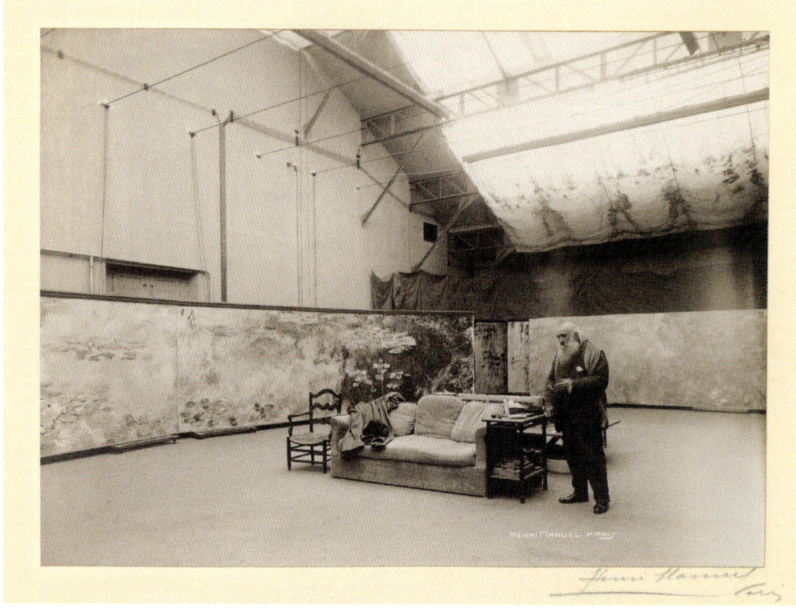


**Fig. 26**
Henri Manuel, *Claude Monet in Front of his Paintings* "The Waterlilies," *in his Studio at Giverny*, 1920, gelatin silver print, Musée Marmottan, Paris, France / Giraudon / The Bridgeman Art Library International (MMT152480)

series of his wintry haystacks—is enough to express the multiple and varied emotions through which passes, from dawn to night, the drama of the earth.

And how many meteoric episodes—towards which the vision of painters had never ventured—has he brought to painting? What shivers of air and wave, what celestial rhythms, atmospheric sonorities, or hazes full of unseen forms has he not rendered?

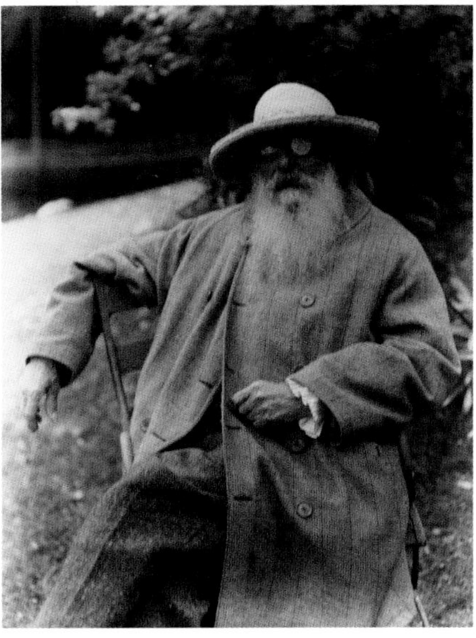

**Fig. 27**
Nickolas Muray, *Claude Monet*, 1926, gelatin silver print, 10 x 8 in. (25.4 x 20.3 cm), Courtesy of George Eastman House, International Museum of Photography and Film, Gift of Mrs. Nickolas Muray (77:0188:2038)

THIS FOR EXAMPLE:

In a skiff resting atop the deep, nearly black water of a shaded river, the banks of which, cut off by the frame, are invisible, two young girls of a charming grace and supple abandon sit fitted in light-colored dresses. The swift current rustles the purple and pink reflections of the dresses through the sun's rays and the shifting reflections of the green leaves. But the drama is not here. In the painting's foreground, made up entirely of the mirrored, brilliant surface of flowing water, the eye penetrates little by little into this wavy freshness all the way to the bed of golden sand beneath and discovers there, through this liquid clarity, an entire life of lake flora, an extraordinary submerged vegetation of long, stringy wild weeds of greenish purple, which, in the flow of the current, flutter, twist, dangle, spread out, and gather up like soft bizarre hairs, then undulate, waver, turn around and extend forth like strange fish, like the fantastic tentacles of marine monsters.

AND THIS:

On a sunny hillside of which we see only the summit of red earth and singed grass, beneath the full sonority of the sky, amidst white and pink clouds which hasten across the azure firmament, a svelte, light, imponderable woman advances, a puff of wind beneath her undulating muslin veil, the lower part of her dress slightly lifted up and stilled by the motion of her step; she appears to hover over the grass. In her modernity, she has the distant grace of a dream, the unexpected charm of an aerial apparition. Look at her closely, for in a moment she will have seemingly passed. In a delicious movement of her arm, the umbrella, which bathes her face in a golden shade, expands like a giant flower. Nothing here of arabesques, but rather simple, straight, and receding lines of an unheard of elegance, of a purity, a sensibility, a breadth of draftsmanship that is truly magisterial and astounding. And this flexible body of a woman, and this dress, the tender shades and bright highlights of which have been melded by the reflections, have combined to make exquisite landscapes of an ineffable cloth.

AND MORE STILL, THIS:

From shadowy mystery, from the shade that bathes her completely, a shade both deep and transparent, a young woman appears, seated and resting her elbows on a lacquer table. Her mauve dress, the contours of which mix and blend into the purple shadows, reveals the nape of her slightly inclined neck and the base of her throat. She is of a delicate and infinitely sad beauty. Enigmatic, with vague eyes, a dangling arm, and the languid and charming attitude of nonchalance, what might she be thinking? We don't know. Has she some problems, some pain, some remorse—what is the secret of her soul? We don't know. She is as strange as the shade that envelops her, which is, like her, troubling and slightly fearsome. But still more strange are these three large sunflowers that emerge from a vase placed near her on the lacquer table, rising up and turning above and in front of her forehead like three ray-less stars of a strange, metallic green, like three stars having come from who knows where to add an eoan mystery, a recessive somberness to the mysterious withdrawal of the ambient shade. The impression is gripping. Involuntarily, it leads one to think of [Edgar Allan Poe's] Ligeia, both ghostly and real, or of one of these women, specters of souls, evoked in the poems of Stéphane Mallarmé.

I imagine that for the public that knows only his admirable landscapes, Claude Monet will have other surprises. For us who know what dreams haunt this great and tirelessly creative mind, these will not be surprises, but indeed the presaged accomplishment, logical and necessary, of projects long entertained; the natural and timely enaction of dreams that haunt this vast genius, for whom, in order to express all that bears expression in life, there will have been only the inability to live the long existence of several human lives. And this is one of his great torments: "We don't have time for anything!" he often says with sadness, he who, still young and full of strength, with a long future full of work still in front of him, is maybe amongst the artists of this century the one whose output is the largest already.

From the *Port of Honfleur* and the *Church Saint-Germain-L'Auxerrois*, a work of such a beautiful, classical aspect, and which reminds one of the purest Canalettos, all the way to the extraordinary haystacks that he completed this winter, what

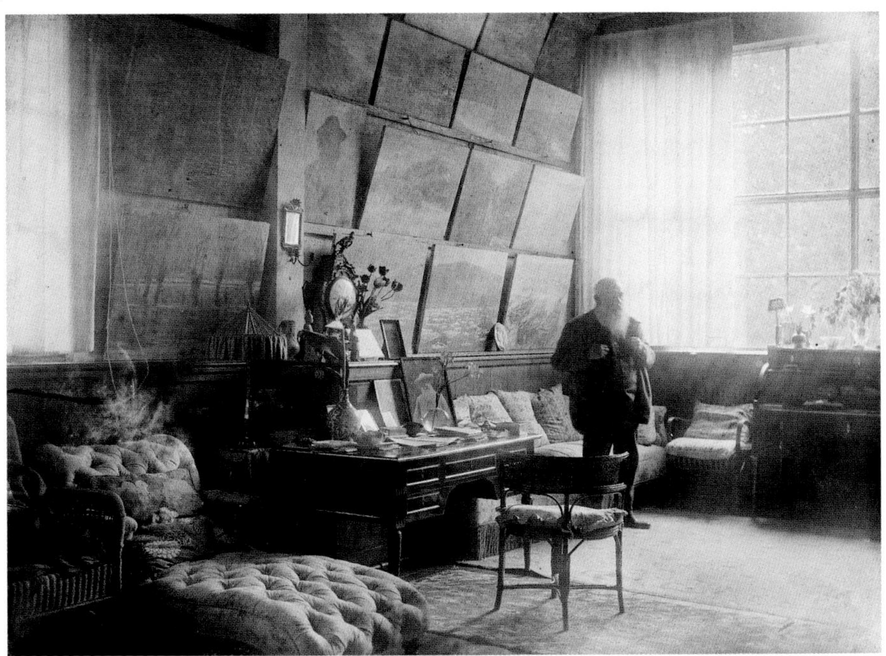

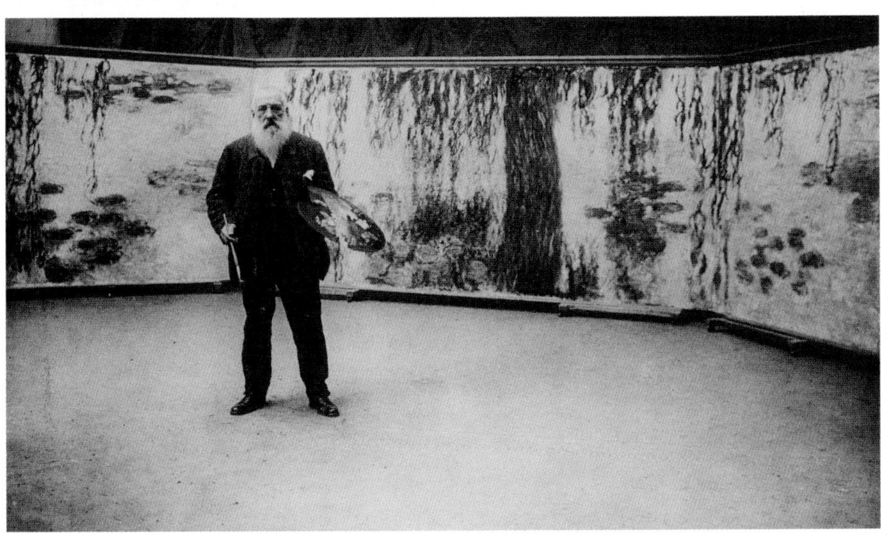

**Fig. 28**
Pierre Choumoff, *Claude Monet in his House at Giverny*, ca. 1915–20, photograph, Roger-Viollet (RV-20141)

**Fig. 29**
Anonymous, *Claude Monet in his Studio at Giverny*, ca. February 1921, photograph, Archives Durand-Ruel (Photo 17172)

a road he has traveled! So many conquests from one year to another! In his upward march, straight, sure, rapid, towards the far side of progress, Claude Monet doesn't have a minute of weakness, not a moment of hesitation or regression. It's a rare thing worthy of the highest admiration, this perpetual upsurge of masterpieces and this superb moral strength that nothing can soften, that nothing can quell. And I love this man, who could now give in to all of the ambitions, vanities, and desires that his celebrity could enable; I love to see him, during a break in his work, with his sleeves rolled up, his hands soiled with compost, his face tanned by the sun, happy to sow seeds in his garden always dazzling with flowers, backed by his cheerful and discreet little house roughcast in pink mortar.

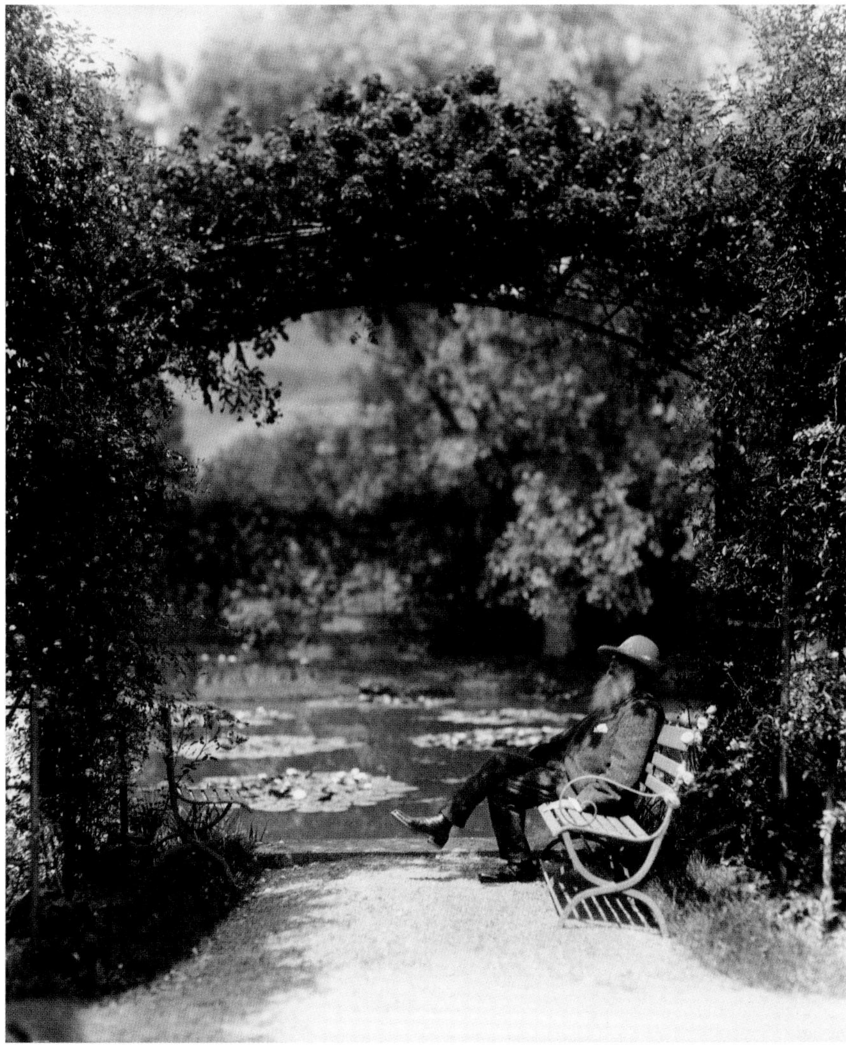

**Fig. 30**
Nickolas Muray, *Monet in his Garden at Giverny, France*, 1926, gelatin silver print, 9 5/8 x 7 11/16 in. (24.4 x 19.5 cm), Courtesy of George Eastman House, International Museum of Photography and Film, Gift of Nickolas Muray Family (77:0188:2039)

# ENDNOTES

### LANDSCAPES, WATERSCAPES, AND REFLECTION IN GIVERNY

1 Monet to Geffroy, August 11, 1908, transcribed in Daniel Wildenstein, *Claude Monet: Biographie et catalogue raisonné* (Lausanne and Paris: La Bibliothèque des Arts, 1979–91), 4:374, no. 1854.

2 Cited in François Thiébault-Sisson, "Les Nymphéas de Claude Monet," *La Revue de l'art ancien et moderne* 52 (July 1927): 44.

3 For a full contextual, philosophical, and historiographic treatment of reflection in terms of the myth of Narcissus in relation to Claude Monet's art see Steven Z. Levine, *Monet, Narcissus, and Self-Reflection* (Chicago and London: The University of Chicago Press, 1994). For a more recent discussion of Monet's adaptations of water themes in his painting see David Clarke, *Water and Art: A Cross-cultural Study of Water as Subject and Medium in Modern and Contemporary Artistic Practice* (London: Reaktion Books, 2010), chapter 2. For reflection in general see Jonathan Miller, *On Reflection* (London: National Gallery Publications Ltd., 1998).

4 P. Larousse, *Nouveau dictionnaire de la langue française* (Paris: Larousse, 1886), 1:650.

5 See notably Paul Hayes Tucker, *Monet in the '90s: The Series Paintings* (New Haven and London: Yale University Press, 1989), 107–41 and "Passion and Patriotism in Monet's Late Work," in Lynn Federle Orr et al., eds., *Monet: Late Paintings of Giverny from the Musée Marmottan* (The Fine Arts Museums of San Francisco, 1994), 19–45. See also the contemporary critic Julien Leclercq, who positions Monet's "lucidity" within a French painting tradition inclusive of the great eighteenth-century painters in "Le Bassin des Nymphéas de Claude Monet," *La Chronique des arts et de la curiosité*, December 1, 1900, 364.

6 John House, *Monet: Nature into Art* (New Haven and London: Yale University Press, 1986), 194.

7 Gaston Bachelard, *Water and Dreams: An Essay on the Imagination of Matter*, trans. Edith R. Farrell (Dallas: The Pegasus Foundation, 1983), 13.

8 Arsène Alexandre, "Le Jardin de Monet," *Le Figaro*, August 9, 1901.

9 Cited in House, *Monet: Nature into Art*, 31.

10 Cited in Thiébault-Sisson, "Les Nymphéas de Claude Monet," 44.

11 Arsène Alexandre, "Les *Nymphéas* de Claude Monet," *Le Figaro*, May 7, 1909.

12 Octave Mirbeau, "Monet et Giverny," *L'Art dans les Deux Mondes*, March 7, 1891. For a translation of the full text, see pp. 72-86 in this volume.

13 Ibid.

14 Yve-Alain Bois, "Cézanne: Words and Deeds," *October* 84 (Spring 1998): 31–43.

15 On Monet, water, and the dryness of Cubism see Clarke, *Water and Art*, 96 ff.

### MIRRORED WATERS

1 *Water and Dreams: An Essay on the Imagination of Matter,* trans. Edith R. Farrell (Dallas: The Pegasus Foundation, 1983), 24.

2 Thiébault-Sisson, "Les Nymphéas de Claude Monet," *La Revue de l'art ancien et moderne* 52 (July 1927), given in John House, *Monet: Nature into Art* (New Haven and London: Yale University Press, 1986), 31.

3 Subtitled *Suivis de réflexions et conseils à un élève sur la peinture, et particulièrement sur le genre du paysage*; 2nd ed. (Paris: Aimé Payen, 1820).

4 Chap. 7, section 6, 157–61; chap. 8, section 6, 175–78; and chap. 9, section 18, 229–30.

5 Valenciennes, *Élémens de perspective*, 158.

6 It states that when a ray of light reflects off a surface, the angle of incidence is equal to the angle of reflection; ibid.

7 Illustrated in Michel Hilaire, Jörg Zutter, and Olivier Zeder, *French Paintings from the Musée Fabre, Montpellier*, exh. cat., National Gallery of Australia, Canberra, and Musée Fabre, Montpellier, Nov. 7, 2003–Feb. 15, 2004, 115.

8 *Metamorphoses*, trans. Frank Justus Miller (London: Heinemann, 1971), I:153.

9 *French Paintings from the Musée Fabre, Montpellier*, cat. entry by Michel Hilaire, 191–92.

10 Peter Galassi, *Corot in Italy* (New Haven and London: Yale University Press, 1991), 69.

11 Ashmolean Museum, Oxford University; illustrated in Gary Tinterow, Michael Pantazzi, and Vincent Pomarède, *Corot*, exh. cat., Metropolitan Museum of Art, New York, Galeries Nationales du Grand Palais, Paris, and National Gallery of Canada, Ottawa, Feb. 27, 1996–Jan. 19, 1997, 72.

12 His peers in Rome reproached him for this. See François Fossier, "Corot in bianco e nero," in Vincent Pomarède, *Corot: natura, emozione, ricordo,* exh. cat., Museo Thyssen-Bornemisza, Madrid, and Palazzo dei Diamanti, Ferrara, June 7, 2005–Jan. 8, 2006, 73.

13 Österreichische Galerie im Belvedere,

Vienna. See reproduction in Tinterow et al., *Corot*, 199.

14 It won wide acclaim and sold to the emperor Napoleon III for 3,000 francs; ibid., 303.

15 Michael Clarke notes that Corot's ephemeral *effets* opened the door to Monet's fugitive *impressions*; *Corot and the Art of Landscape* (New York: Abbeville Press, 1991), chap. 6, "Corot and Impressionism," 109.

16 Étienne Moreau-Nélaton, *Daubigny raconté par lui-même* (Paris: Henri Laurens, 1925), 73.

17 Correspondence with paintings conservator Charlotte Seifen Ameringer, Fine Arts Museums of San Francisco, based on a laboratory examination of August 15, 2002.

18 "Les Daubignys sont pour moi quelque chose de bien beau," Paris, May 19, 1859, my translation; Daniel Wildenstein, *Claude Monet: Biographie et catalogue raisonné* (Lausanne and Paris: La Bibliothèque des Arts, 1979–91), 419.

19 Larry Keith and Raymond White, "Mixed Media in the Work of Charles-François Daubigny: Analysis and Implications for Conservation," *National Gallery Technical Bulletin* 23 (2002): 42–48.

20 Mark Haworth-Booth makes a similar point about early French photographs of rivers in *Camille Silvy: River Scene, France* (Malibu, Calif.: The J. Paul Getty Museum, 1992), 107.

21 Daniel Wildenstein, *Monet or the Triumph of Impressionism* (Paris: Wildenstein Institute and Cologne: Taschen, 1996), I:98.

22 They likely met in the late summer of 1864 in Honfleur, when Monet was painting with Johan Barthold Jongkind and met other painters, reportedly including Daubigny, at Mère Toutain's inn at the Saint-Siméon farm; *Jongkind (1819–1891)*, exh. cat., Gementemuseum, The Hague, Wallraf-Richartz-Museum, Cologne, and Musée d'Orsay, Paris, Oct. 11, 2003–Sept. 5, 2004, 220. They assuredly knew each other by 1868, when both exhibited (and received medals) at the Le Havre International Maritime Exhibition along with Courbet, Manet, and Pissarro; Wildenstein, *Monet or the Triumph of Impressionism*, I:40.

23 For examples, see Monet's *Régates à Argenteuil*, ca. 1872, Musée d'Orsay, Paris; and *Autumn Effect at Argenteuil*, 1873, Courtauld Institute Gallery, London.

24 It has been plausibly suggested that the work was painted in Saintonge, in southwestern France, during Courbet's stay there in 1862, when he informed his dealer Luquet that he was planning to deliver thirty-three canvases painted there and made suggestions on how to market them. Very likely, the inclusion of the graceful deer signaled Courbet's commercial intentions for the canvas; Sarah Faunce and Linda Nochlin, *Courbet Reconsidered*, exh. cat., Brooklyn Museum and Minneapolis Institute of Arts, Nov. 4, 1988–Apr. 30, 1989, cat. entry by Ann Dumas, 142. See also Mary Morton and Charlotte Eyerman, *Courbet and the Modern Landscape*, exh. cat., The J. Paul Getty Museum, Los Angeles, Museum of Fine Arts, Houston, and Walters Art Museum, Baltimore, Oct. 15, 2006–Jan. 7, 2007, 67.

25 A handy visual compendium of the best of the over two dozen versions of this subject are reproduced in Mary Morton's essay "Forests and Streams," in Morton and Eyerman, *Courbet and the Modern Landscape*, 66–80.

26 *The Shaded Stream at the Puits Noir,* The Baltimore Museum of Art; reproduced in ibid., 77.

27 There are documented visits to Paris in 1865, and to Le Havre in 1868; Courbet was a witness at Monet's wedding in 1870. Wildenstein, *Monet or the Triumph of Impressionism,* I:59, 70, 80.

28 Monet undoubtedly saw the Musée d'Orsay version of the Puits Noir, *The Shaded Stream*, at the Salon of 1865; illustrated in Morton and Eyerman, *Courbet and the Modern Landscape*, 75.

29 For example, Daubigny repeated the motif in an 1861 Salon submission, *Un village près de Bonnières*, 1861, illustrated in Gary Tinterow and Henri Loyrette, *The Origins of Impressionism,* exh. cat., Galeries Nationales du Grand Palais, Paris, and Metropolitan Museum of Art, New York, Apr. 10, 1994–Jan. 8, 1995, 87; and in a variant from the same year at the Taft Museum of Art, Cincinnati, illustrated in *The Taft Museum: European and American Paintings* (New York: Hudson Hills Press, 1995), 267.

30 He liked the area so much that he returned later to settle in nearby Giverny. Wildenstein, *Monet or the Triumph of Impressionism*, I:70, and II:56. Cézanne had also stayed in Gloton in 1866.

31 In other paintings, however, Monet showed both objects and their reflections; see the examples compiled by David Clarke, *Water and Art: A Cross-cultural Study of Water*

*as Subject and Medium in Modern and Contemporary Artistic Practice* (London: Reaktion Books, 2010), chap. 2, "Monet and the Surface of Water," 89.

32 He rendered a few river scenes with still water in Argenteuil in 1872, 1873, and 1874; Wildenstein, *Monet or the Triumph of Impressionism*, I, nos. 233, 290, 291, and 323.

33 The most enlightened guide to Monet's technique during this period remains Robert Herbert, "Method and Meaning in Monet," *Art in America* 67, 5 (September 1979): 90–108.

34 On Monet and moving water, see Clarke, *Water and Art*, 78–85.

35 Wildenstein, *Monet or the Triumph of Impressionism*, III, nos. 1472–1493.

36 House, *Monet: Nature into Art*, following writers contemporary to Monet, 30. For one, Lila Cabot Perry pointed out the similarities in 1927 and suggested that Monet was conscious of them.

37 Tinterow et al., *Corot*, xiv, from a 1927 account by Raymond Koechlin: "Il n'y en a qu'un ici, c'est Corot; nous, nous ne sommes rien, rien, près de lui!"

38 Monet to Gustave Geffroy in 1922; Wildenstein, *Monet or the Triumph of Impressionism*, I: 383.

### FRAGMENTS AND REFLECTIONS

1 The author wishes to thank Franny Brock, Selina Bartlett, Anne Buening, and Benedict Leca, and to acknowledge Joel Isaacson's entry on Oberlin's *Wisteria* painting for the Allen Memorial Art Museum's 1998 CD-ROM.
Maurice Guillemot, "Claude Monet," *La Revue Illustrée*, March 15, 1898, as trans. in Charles Stuckey, *Monet: A Retrospective* (New York: Hugh Lauter Levin Associates, 1985), 200, on his August 1897 visit to Giverny: "...these are the models for a decoration, for which he has already begun to paint studies, large panels, which he showed me afterward in his studio. Imagine a circular room in which the dado beneath the molding is covered with [paintings of] water, dotted with these plants to the very horizon, walls of a transparency alternately green and mauve, the calm and silence of the still waters reflecting the opened blossoms."

2 The idea for a large decorative project was noted by two reviewers of the May–June 1909 exhibition of *Water Lilies* at Durand-Ruel. Roger Marx, "Les 'Nymphéas' de M. Claude Monet," *Gazette des Beaux-Arts*, 51e année, 1er semestre (June 1909): 529, in an imaginary conversation, has Monet say, "Un moment la tentation m'est venue d'employer à la décoration d'un salon ce thème des nymphéas: transporté le long des murs, enveloppant toutes les parois de son unité, il aurait procuré l'illusion d'un tout sans fin, d'une onde sans horizon et sans rivage; les nerfs surmenés par le travail se seraient détendus là, selon l'exemple reposant de ces eaux stagnantes, et, à qui l'eût habitée, cette pièce aurait offert l'asile d'une méditation paisible au centre d'un aquarium fleuri." Arsène Alexandre, "Un Paysagiste d'aujourd'hui et un portraitiste de jadis," *Comoedia*, May 8, 1909, trans. in Paul Hayes Tucker, *Claude Monet: Life and Art* (New Haven and London: Yale University Press, 1995), 235, note 30, wrote that Monet had a dream of decorating "a circular room of modest, well-calculated dimensions...Around it, to half human height, there would...extend a painting of water and flowers."

3 Duc de Trévise, "Pilgrimage to Giverny," *La Revue de l'art ancien et moderne* (special ed., 1927): 27, writing about two visits to Giverny in 1920, as trans. in Stuckey, *Monet: A Retrospective*, 339–40: "...it does seem to me that the owner of one of your series would not have anything to complain about. It wouldn't require a great deal of imagination to erect on his lawn a spacious pavilion to house the paintings; above them would be the calm gray of walls, surmounted by some sort of flowered frieze...' 'That's precisely what I had in mind; I'll even show you the first garlands for the frieze; I am using wisteria for it.'" François Thiébault-Sisson, "A Gift of Claude Monet to the State," *Le Temps*, October 14, 1920, as trans. in Stuckey, *Monet: A Retrospective*, 304, also wrote about the Hôtel de Biron plans that "the glazed ceiling will be sufficiently high to accommodate a wide enough space for decorative motifs, between the lower edge of the window and the top of the canvases, which M. Claude Monet will furnish and which will separate the series."

4 Among many publications citing the steps he took to divert the Ru stream and all the concomitant work involved in the creation of the garden, is Tucker, *Claude Monet: Life and Art*, 175–78, 188.

5 Elizabeth Murray in Lynn Federle Orr et al., eds., *Monet: Late Paintings of Giverny from the Musée Marmottan* (The Fine Arts

Museums of San Francisco, 1994), 57. She notes that he combined Japanese and Chinese strains of wisteria for a longer growing period.

6 Adding to his sadness of the time, Monet's wife Alice had died in 1911 and his elder son Jean in February 1914. Claire Joyes, *Claude Monet: Life at Giverny* (London: Thames and Hudson, 1985), 108; Tucker, *Claude Monet: Life and Art*, 205–6; Paul Hayes Tucker et al., *Monet in the 20th Century* (Boston: Museum of Fine Arts, and London: Royal Academy of Arts, 1998), 65–67; this last, 64–85, is, along with Robert Gordon and Charles F. Stuckey, "Blossoms and Blunders: Monet and the State," *Art in America* 67 (January–February 1979, 102–17 and September 1979, 109–25), among the best publications on Monet and the First World War.

7 François Thiébault-Sisson, "Claude Monet: An Interview," *Le Temps*, November 27, 1900, as trans. in Stuckey, *Monet: A Retrospective*, 206. See also Tucker, *Claude Monet: Life and Art*, 17–18. He left the army early, in 1862, as he became ill, and subsequently his family purchased his release owing to a recently enacted law that enabled this. Thiébault-Sisson, "About Claude Monet," *Le Temps*, December 29, 1926, as trans. in Stuckey, *Monet: A Retrospective*, 342, writes of anecdotes he heard either from Monet or from Clemenceau that Monet thought of Algeria as "a country that had left me with so many awful memories," but nonetheless, his military service would not nearly have been as onerous as the active fighting in the Franco-Prussian War and the First World War.

8 Tucker, *Claude Monet: Life and Art*, 35, 46–47. Denis Rouart, in Denis Rouart and Léon Degand, *Claude Monet* (Lausanne: Éditions d'Art Albert Skira, 1958), 50, writes of the many early works by Monet, stored with Pissarro in Louveciennes, which were torn from their frames and used as aprons and floor-mats, when the Germans advanced there and turned Pissarro's house into a regimental butcher's shop. Monet's friend the painter Bazille was killed in action in November 1870.

9 Tucker, *Monet in the 20th Century*, 64–65, 289 notes 197–98. He notes that it was most likely mid-late May 1914 when Monet started his canvases.

10 Tucker, *Claude Monet: Life and Art*, 236, note 54. François Thiébault-Sisson, "Claude Monet's Water Lilies," *La Revue de l'art ancien et moderne* 52 (July 1927), as trans. in Stuckey, *Monet: A Retrospective*, 290–91, writes of a visit to the artist in early February 1918, in which Monet informed him he had decided in early 1914 to return to painting after a period of discouragement because of his eye problems, and, despite his cataract, to "create a kind of synthesis, a kind of summing up, in one or perhaps two canvases, of all my former impressions and feelings...I said to myself that a series of impressions of the ensemble [of my pond]...would be of some interest...I made up my mind to act, and I acted. I've always been a decisive man once I've made up my mind. On the spot, I sent for the mason... We drew up a plan...for an unusually large studio...The workmen began digging the foundations on the first of August. Then came the general mobilization and the war...It wasn't finished until the spring of 1916. Then, when the work was barely completed, I set to work. In two years I have completed eight of the twelve panels that I had planned to do, and the other four are now underway." It is clear that Monet's desire to start the great project predated the war, but there is an insistence on mentioning that the construction of the studio began on August 1, 1914. A second remembrance, this by the Duc de Trévise, confirms that Monet began the project to pull himself out of depression caused by the deaths of his wife and son, and his cataract; writing in "Pilgrimage to Giverny," *La Revue de l'art ancien et moderne*, January–February 1927, as trans. in Stuckey, *Monet: A Retrospective*, 338, he notes that "After the tragedy of my life and after my illness, I stopped painting...I had the beginning of a cataract...It was my old friend Clemenceau who pulled me through my bereavement. I discussed with him a kind of decoration I once wanted to do. He said, 'That's a superb project! You can still do it—do it!' And I did." Additionally, in June 1914 Félix Fénéon published a letter from Monet declining an invitation to Paris because of involvement in a "grand travail," as noted in Daniel Wildenstein, *Monet's Years at Giverny: Beyond Impressionism* (New York: Metropolitan Museum of Art, 1978), 169.

11 Louis Gillet, *Trois variations sur Claude Monet* (Paris: Plon, 1927), 77–78, as noted in William C. Seitz, *Claude Monet: Seasons and Moments* (New York: The Museum of Modern Art, 1960), 46.

12 Tucker, *Claude Monet: Life and Art*, 212. As Tucker notes, he would need to post-date them to coincide with the Armistice.

13 Ibid., 225.

14 Ellen Johnson, *Fragments Recalled at Eighty: The Art Memoirs of Ellen H. Johnson*, ed. Athena Tacha (North Vancouver: Gallerie, 1993), 52. Johnson compiled the memoirs from 1989 to 1991; as Tacha notes in her introduction, 14, "It is…a text about memory and the act of recalling." René Gimpel, in his *Journal*, as trans. in Stuckey, *Monet: A Retrospective*, 312, wrote of Blanche Hoschedé, on July 17, 1923, being "fed up with" Michel Monet, who didn't work and was "very spoiled by his father."

15 Seitz, *Claude Monet: Seasons and Moments*, 50. For the shell damage at the Orangerie, see among other publications Virginia Spate, *Claude Monet: Life and Work* (New York: Rizzoli, 1992), 316, 334 note 126.

16 Hoschedé was born August 20, 1877 and was seventy-three when Johnson met him. The youngest of Monet's six stepchildren, he liked in later life to refer to his physical resemblance to Monet and some scholars believe he may have been Monet's child. See Sylvie Patin, *Monet, The Ultimate Impressionist* (New York: Harry N. Abrams, Inc., 1993), 50.

17 Marcel Proust, *Du côté de chez Swann*, vol. 1 of *À la recherche du temps perdu* (Paris: Gallimard, 1919, printed for Québec: Les Éditions Variétés, 1944), 69–73. He writes, 73, both of "l'odeur et la saveur" engendering recollection, and of "les nymphéas de la Vivonne" as among the memories recalled. The river was in actuality the Loir, but was poetically renamed Vivonne in his works. Proust earlier had written of Monet's gardens, with their "earth flowers and also water flowers," in "'Les Éblouissements' par la comtesse de Noailles," *Le Figaro*, June 15, 1907, literary supplement.

18 Jay Gorney, "Oberlin's Tribute to Ellen Johnson," *Art News* 74, no. 4 (April 1975): 34, also quoted by Richard Spear in "Ellen H. Johnson, 1910–1992" in Johnson, *Fragments Recalled at Eighty*, 7.

19 Johnson, *Fragments Recalled at Eighty*, 61.

20 Charles Parkhurst, Allen Memorial Art Museum director, was in correspondence with Alexandre Rosenberg at Paul Rosenberg & Co., in September 1959, regarding Oberlin's purchase. Rosenberg indicated that the painting had been in Michel Monet's collection, and secured through Katia Granoff, though she had not owned it (corres. in museum files). E. A. Carmean, Jr., "Morris Louis and the Modern Tradition: II. Cubism, III. Impressionism," *Arts Magazine* 51, no. 2 (October 1976): 117, note 12, writes that "Charles Parkhurst, who was instrumental in Oberlin's acquisition of *Wisteria*, has recounted to me how radical the painting appeared to most people when Oberlin was considering its purchase in the late 1950s." Ellsworth Kelly visited Giverny in September 1952, and he too was bowled over by what he saw, as well as the disrepair into which the site had fallen; see James Yood, "Making Monet Matter: Giverny and Modern Art," in *In Monet's Garden: Artists and the Lure of Giverny* (Columbus, Ohio: Columbus Museum of Art, 2007), 97. Among the best publications on renewed interest in Monet in the 1950s is Michael Leja, "The Monet Revival and New York School Abstraction," in Tucker, *Monet in the 20th Century*, 98–108. For Katia Granoff's promotion of Monet's late works, see Leja, "The Monet Revival," 100, and Joseph Baillio, "Katia Granoff (1895–1989): Champion of the Late Works of Claude Monet," in *Claude Monet (1840–1926): A Tribute to Daniel Wildenstein and Katia Granoff* (New York: Wildenstein, 2007), 35–44.

21 Monet maintained, according to Maurice Kahn, "Claude Monet's Garden," *Le Temps* (June 7, 1904), as trans. in Stuckey, *Monet: A Retrospective*, 244, that the resemblance of his garden and bridge to Japanese precedents "is quite unintentional." Yet the importance of Japanese art for his own life's work, and for his garden design, has been amply written about by other scholars; see Virginia Spate, Gary Hickey, David Bromfield et al. *Monet & Japan* (Canberra: National Gallery of Australia, 2001).

### FROM INSTANT TO *ENVELOPPE*

1 The complicated relationship between the Impressionists—and Monet, especially—and the (mis)application of Chevreul's theories in their work is discussed at length in Georges Roque, "Chevreul and Impressionism: A Reappraisal," *The Art Bulletin* 78 (March 1996): 26–39.

2 Aaron Scharf, *Art and Photography* (London: Penguin Books, 1968), 170–72.

3 Monet to Durand-Ruel, February 12, 1905, quoted in Jacqueline and Maurice Guillard,

*Claude Monet at the Time of Giverny* (Paris: Centre Culturel du Marais, 1983), 283.

4 The best source describing this development in detail is John House, *Monet: Nature into Art* (New Haven and London: Yale University Press, 1986).

5 On Muybridge's direct contribution to Edison's invention of the motion picture, see Rebecca Solnit, *River of Shadows: Eadweard Muybridge and the Technological Wild West* (New York: Viking Penguin, 2003), 228–31.

6 Monet to Geffroy, October 7, 1890, quoted in House, *Monet: Nature into Art*, 220.

# BIBLIOGRAPHY


Alexandre, Arsène. "Le Jardin de Monet." *Le Figaro*, August 9, 1901.

______. "Les *Nymphéas* de Claude Monet." *Le Figaro*, May 7, 1909.

Bachelard, Gaston. *Water and Dreams: An Essay on the Imagination of Matter.* Translated by Edith R. Farrell. Dallas: The Pegasus Foundation, 1983.

Baillio, Joseph. "Katia Granoff (1895–1989): Champion of the Late Works of Claude Monet." In *Claude Monet (1840–1926): A Tribute to Daniel Wildenstein and Katia Granoff*, 35–44. New York: Wildenstein, 2007. An exhibition catalog.

Clarke, David. *Water and Art: A Cross-cultural Study of Water as Subject and Medium in Modern and Contemporary Artistic Practice.* London: Reaktion Books, 2010.

Gordon, Robert, and Charles F. Stuckey. "Blossoms and Blunders: Monet and the State." *Art in America* 67 (1979): 102–17.

Greenberg, Clement. "The Later Monet." *Art News Annual* 26 (1957): 132–48 and 194–99.

Guillard, Jacqueline and Maurice. *Claude Monet au temps de Giverny / Claude Monet at the Time of Giverny*. Paris: Centre Culturel du Marais, 1983. An exhibition catalog.

Hoog, Michel. *Les Nymphéas de Claude Monet au Musée de l'Orangerie*. Paris: Éditions de la Réunion des musées nationaux, 1984.

House, John. *Monet: Nature into Art*. New Haven and London: Yale University Press, 1986.

______, and Virginia Spate. *Claude Monet: Painter of Light*. Auckland: City Art Gallery, in association with NZI Corporation, 1985. An exhibition catalog.

Isaacson, Joel. *Claude Monet: Observation and Reflection*. Oxford: Phaidon, 1978.

Johnson, Ellen. *Fragments Recalled at Eighty: The Art Memoirs of Ellen H. Johnson*. Edited by Athena Tacha. North Vancouver: Gallerie, 1993.

Joyes, Claire. *Monet at Giverny*. London: Mathews Miller Dunbar Ltd., 1975.

______. *Claude Monet: Life at Giverny*. London: Thames and Hudson, 1985.

Levine, Steven Z. *Monet, Narcissus, and Self-Reflection*. Chicago and London: The University of Chicago Press, 1994.

Miller, Jonathan. *On Reflection*. London: National Gallery Publications Ltd., 1998.

Murray, Elizabeth. "Monet as a Garden Artist." In *Monet: Late Paintings of Giverny from the Musée Marmottan*. Edited by Lynn Federle Orr et al., 47–60. The Fine Arts Museums of San Francisco, in association with H.N. Abrams, 1994. An exhibition catalog.

Orr, Lynn Federle, Paul Hayes Tucker, and Elizabeth Murray, *Monet: Late Paintings of Giverny from the Musée Marmottan*. The Fine Arts Museums of San Francisco, in association with H.N. Abrams, 1994. An exhibition catalog.

Patin, Sylvie. *Monet: The Ultimate Impressionist.* New York: Harry N. Abrams, Inc., 1993.

Rouart, Denis, and Léon Degand. *Claude Monet*. Lansanne: Éditions d'Art Albert Skira, 1958.

______, and Jean-Dominique Rey. *Monet, nymphéas; ou, Les miroirs du temps* (includes catalogue raisonné by Robert Maillard). Paris: F. Hazan, 1972.

Scharf, Aaron. *Art and Photography.* London: Penguin Books, 1968.

Seitz, William C. *Claude Monet: Seasons and Moments*. New York: The Museum of Modern Art, and Los Angeles: Los Angeles County Museum, in association with Garden City, N.Y., 1960. An exhibition catalog.

Solnit, Rebecca. *River of Shadows: Eadweard Muybridge and the Technological Wild West.* New York: Viking Penguin, 2003.

Spate, Virginia. *Claude Monet: Life and Work.* New York: Rizzoli, 1992.

Spate, Virginia, Gary Hickey, David Bromfield et al. *Monet & Japan.* Canberra: National Gallery of Australia, and Perth: The Art Gallery of Northern Australia, in association with the University of Washington Press, 2001. An exhibition catalog.

Stuckey, Charles F. "Blossoms and Blunders: Monet and the State II." *Art in America* 67 (1979): 109–25.

______, editor. *Monet: A Retrospective*. New York: Hugh Lauter Levin Associates, Inc., 1985.

Thiébault-Sisson, François. "Les Nymphéas de Claude Monet." *La Revue de l'art ancien et moderne* 52 (July 1927): 41–51.

Tucker, Paul Hayes. *Monet in the '90s: The Series Paintings*. Boston: Museum of Fine Arts, in association with Yale University Press, 1989. An exhibition catalog.

______. "Passion and Patriotism in Monet's Late Work." In *Monet: Late Paintings of Giverny from the Musée Marmottan*. Edited by Lynn Federle Orr et al., 29–46. The Fine Arts Museums of San Francisco, in association with H.N. Abrams, 1994. An exhibition catalog.

______. *Claude Monet: Life and Art.* New Haven and London: Yale University Press, 1995.

______, George T.M. Shackelford, and MaryAnne Stevens. *Monet in the 20th Century*. Boston: Museum of Fine Arts, and London: Royal Academy of Arts, in association with Yale University Press, 1998. An exhibition catalog.

______. *Claude Monet: Late Work.* New York: Gagosian Gallery, in association with Rizzoli, 2010. An exhibition catalog.

Wildenstein, Daniel. *Monet's Years at Giverny: Beyond Impressionism*. New York: Metropolitan Museum of Art, 1978. An exhibition catalog.

______. *Claude Monet: Biographie et catalogue raisonné.* Lausanne and Paris: La Bibliothèque des Arts, 1979–91.

______. *Monet or the Triumph of Impressionism.* Paris: Wildenstein Institute and Cologne: Taschen, 1996.

Yood, James. "Making Monet Matter: Giverny and Modern Art." In *Monet's Garden: Artists and the Lure of Giverny*, 95–157. Columbus, Ohio: Columbus Museum of Art, and Paris: Musée Marmottan, in association with Scala Publishers, 2007. An exhibition catalog.

# PHOTOGRAPHIC CREDITS

**Catalog Plates**

Cat. 3 Photograph © 2012 Museum of Fine Arts, Boston
Cat. 7 Photograph courtesy of the Denver Art Museum
Cat. 9 Jean Paul Torno
Cat. 12 Jean Paul Torno

**Benedict Leca, Landscapes, Waterscapes, and Reflection in Giverny**

Fig. 1 © Collection Philippe Piguet, Paris
Fig. 2 © The Samuel Courtauld Trust, The Courtauld Gallery, London

**Lynne D. Ambrosini, Mirrored Waters: Reflections on Monet and his Predecessors**

Fig. 4 Erich Lessing / Art Resource, NY
Fig. 5 © Fine Arts Museums of San Francisco
Fig. 6 Photo: The Montreal Museum of Fine Arts, Christine Guest
Fig. 7 Photograph © 2012 Museum of Fine Arts, Boston
Fig. 8 Photography © The Art Institute of Chicago

**Beth E. Wilson, From Instant to *Enveloppe*: Reflections on Monet, Photography, and Time**

Fig. 13 Jamison Miller

**Octave Mirbeau, Monet and Giverny**

Fig. 16 Réunion des Musées Nationaux / Art Resource, NY
Fig. 18 © Durand-Ruel & Cie, all rights reserved
Fig. 19 © Durand-Ruel & Cie, all rights reserved
Fig. 20 Réunion des Musées Nationaux / Art Resource, NY
Fig. 21 Réunion des Musées Nationaux / Art Resource, NY
Fig. 22 © Nickolas Muray Photo Archives
Fig. 24 © Nickolas Muray Photo Archives
Fig. 25 © Collection Philippe Piguet, Paris
Fig. 27 © Nickolas Muray Photo Archives
Fig. 28 © Pierre Choumoff / Roger-Viollet
Fig. 29 © Durand-Ruel & Cie, all rights reserved
Fig. 30 © Nickolas Muray Photo Archives

# INDEX

Pages numbers in *italics* indicate illustrations. All illustrations are of works by Monet unless otherwise indicated